DORLING KINDERSLEY DK EYEWITNESS BOOKS

MEDICINE

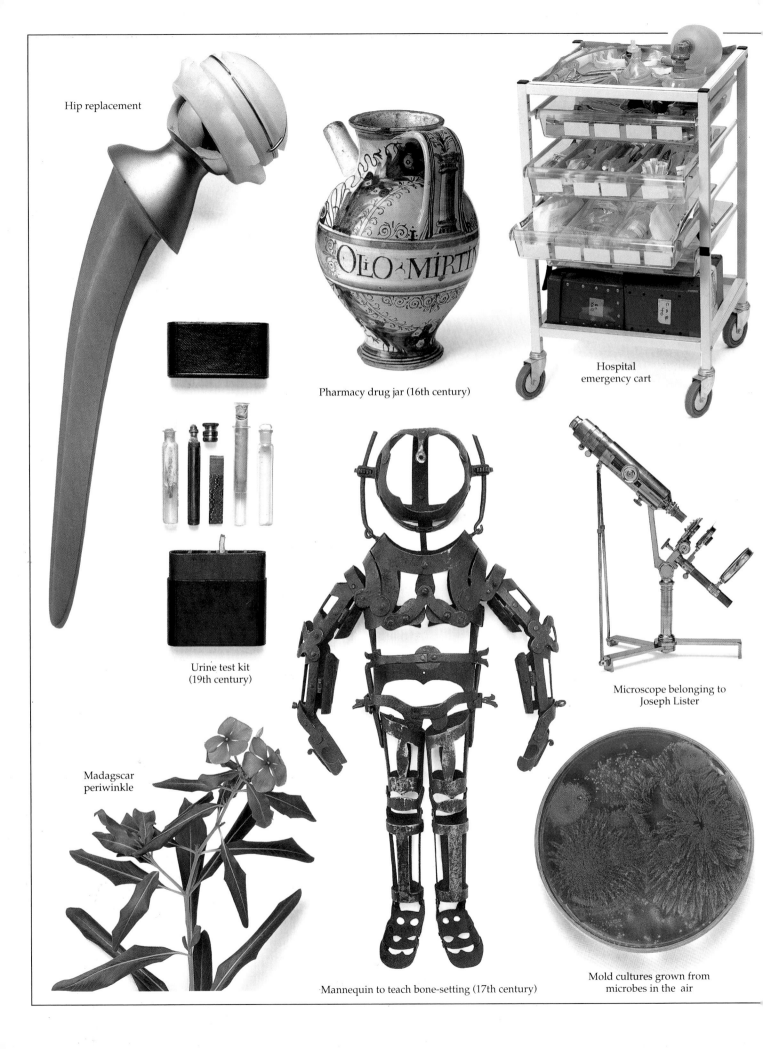

Hip replacement

Pharmacy drug jar (16th century)

OLiO·MIRTIN

Hospital emergency cart

Urine test kit (19th century)

Microscope belonging to Joseph Lister

Madagscar periwinkle

Mannequin to teach bone-setting (17th century)

Mold cultures grown from microbes in the air

56 ARCHEOLOGY
57 ARCTIC & ANTARCTIC
58 BUILDING
59 PIRATE
60 NORTH AMERICAN INDIAN
61 AFRICA
62 OCEAN

63 BATTLE
64 GORILLA, MONKEY & APE
65 MEDIEVAL LIFE
66 FARM
67 SPY
68 RELIGION
69 EAGLE & BIRDS OF PREY

70 WITCHES & MAGIC-MAKERS
71 SPACE EXPLORATION
72 SHIPWRECK
73 CRIME & DETECTION
74 RUSSIA
75 LIGHT
76 ENERGY

77 ELECTRICITY
78 FORCE & MOTION
79 CHEMISTRY
80 MATTER
81 TIME & SPACE
82 ASTRONOMY
83 EARTH

84 LIFE
85 EVOLUTION
86 ECOLOGY
87 HUMAN BODY
88 MEDICINE
89 TECHNOLOGY
90 ELECTRONICS

91 RENAISSANCE
92 IMPRESSIONISM
93 GOYA
94 MANET
95 MONET
96 VAN GOGH
97 WATERCOLOR

98 PERSPECTIVE
99 DANCE
100 FUTURE
101 MYTHOLOGY
102 LEONARDO & HIS TIMES
103 OLYMPICS
104 MEDIA & COMMUNICATION

105 TITANIC
106 FOOTBALL
107 HURRICANE & TORNADO
108 SOCCER
109 PRESIDENTS
110 BASEBALL

WITHDRAWN

Artificial heart valves

EYEWITNESS BOOKS

Vaccination lancet
(19th century)

MEDICINE

Disposable one-shot syringe

Written by
STEVE PARKER

Contraceptive pills

Leeches and leech cage
(18th century)

Italian
anatomical
figures
(17th century)

Petit tourniquet
(18th century)

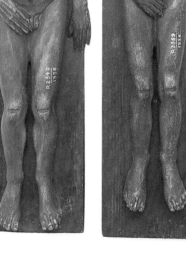

DK
Dorling Kindersley

Straitjacket (1930s)

Model of an instrument sterilizing unit

Stethometer
to measure
chest expansion

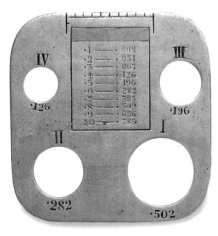

Gauge to measure size of smallpox pustules

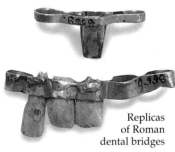

Replicas
of Roman
dental bridges

Fennel

DK

Dorling Kindersley
LONDON, NEW YORK, AUCKLAND, DELHI, JOHANNESBURG,
MUNICH, PARIS and SYDNEY

For a full catalog, visit
 www.dk.com

Project editor Antonia Cunningham
Art editor Thomas Keenes
Designer Elaine C. Monaghan
Production Catherine Toque
Picture research Deborah Pownall
and Becky Halls
Managing editor Josephine Buchanan
Managing art editor Lynne Brown
Special photography David Exton, John Lepine,
Adrian Whicher, and Jane Stockman
Editorial consultants Timothy Boon
and Ghislaine Lawrence
US editor Ray Rogers
US consultant James H. Weir, M.D.

This Eyewitness ® Book has been conceived by
Dorling Kindersley Limited and Editions Gallimard

© 1995 Dorling Kindersley Limited
This edition © 2000 Dorling Kindersley Limited
First American edition, 1995

Published in the United States by
Dorling Kindersley Publishing, Inc.
95 Madison Avenue
New York, NY 10016
2 4 6 8 10 9 7 5 3 1

Dorling Kindersley books are available at special
discounts for bulk purchases for sales promotions or
premiums. Special editions, including personalized
covers, excerpts of existing guides, and corporate imprints can be
created in large quantities for specific needs. For more
information, contact Special Markets Dept., Dorling Kindersley
Publishing, Inc., 95 Madison Ave., New York, NY 10016;
Fax: (800) 600-9098

Library of Congress Cataloging-in-Publication Data
Parker, Steve.
Medicine / written by Steve Parker.
p. cm — (Eyewitness Books)
1. Medicine — Juvenile literature. [1. Medicine.]
I. Title. II. Series.
R130.5.P37   2000
610—dc20   94-34860
                                                      CIP
                                                       AC
ISBN 0-7894-6173-0 (pb)
ISBN 0-7894-5580-3 (hc)

Color reproduction by Colourscan, Singapore
Printed in China by Toppan Printing Co. (Shenzhen) Ltd.

Antiseptic machine (19th century)

Mask
belonging to
Iroquois Indians

Enema syringe (18th century)

False metal nose (16th century)

Contents

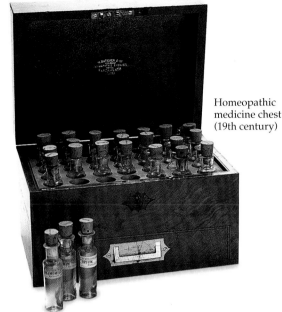

Homeopathic medicine chest (19th century)

What is medicine?

THROUGHOUT HISTORY, PEOPLE HAVE tried to cure illness and restore health. It is an instinct that applies even to animals. Healing remedies have taken a huge variety of forms from preparations using plants, animals, and minerals to removal of infected or diseased parts, to prayers or incantations for spirits or gods to restore health. Today the Western health professions involve numerous specialists, equipment, buildings, and organizations. In many countries, the health and medical service is the biggest employer and spends more money than any other industry. Views vary as to what should be considered as medicine. In the West, first, at least in theory, is prevention – trying to lead healthy lives by eating healthy food, exercising, and avoiding accident and disease (by immunization for example, p. 32). If a person is ill, the signs and symptoms of illness are followed by diagnosis of the problem and its cause, and treatment. But there are many gray areas and different viewpoints about what constitutes medicine, what is effective and safe, what is worth doing, and what is acceptable in terms of research, experimentation, and cost.

INSTINCTIVE MEDICINE
Some tendencies in medicine seem to be built in, for animals as well as people. Animals follow their instincts when ill – they lie down, drink, eat certain foods, and vomit. Gorillas in West Africa intentionally eat several types of plant that are effective against intestinal worms, joint pains, and other conditions.

EXPECTATIONS OF MEDICINE
People in developed countries have relatively high expectations of health and medicine. They view illness as something out of the ordinary that should quickly be cured by the advanced medical services. In other areas of the world, such as parts of the Philippines, shown above, infection and illness are a way of life, and a healthier existence is an unlikely dream. A general rise in expectations has also occurred over time, as people in the developed world expect to lead longer and healthier lives. What might people in the future come to expect?

Nails

Mirror

SYSTEMS OF MEDICINE
In some cultures, medicine is concerned less with scientific tests and hi-tech advances that treat the physical body, and more with the comfort of the inner soul and its relationship with the spirit world. This fetish figure from the Congo, in central Africa, comes from the Yombe or a neighboring tribe. Driving nails into the effigy during the appropriate ceremony or ritual is intended to cause disease and death or drive illness from the part of the body in which the nail or nails are inserted.

CHEMICAL MEDICINE

Modern medicine's chief weapons against disease are drugs and surgery. A drug is any substance or chemical that affects the functions of the body. The first drugs were in plants and animal products used in ancient times. In 1785 the English physician William Withering (1741-1799) wrote *An Account of the Foxglove*, a description of how to use the plant to treat dropsy. In this condition fluid accumulates in the body tissues, usually due to heart or circulatory problems. In small doses the plant was helpful, causing heart stimulation, but in larger amounts it was harmful and even fatal. Withering's work was one of the first scientific accounts of drug use in modern times. Further research showed that the important chemical in foxglove is digitalis. Derivatives of this substance are still used to treat heart failure.

Ear piece

Binaural (two-ear) stethoscope

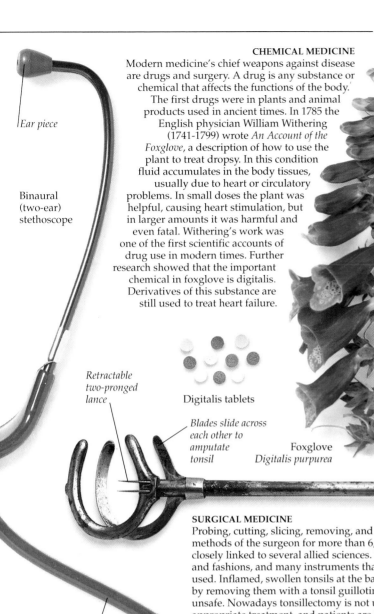

Retractable two-pronged lance

Digitalis tablets

Blades slide across each other to amputate tonsil

Foxglove
Digitalis purpurea

IS IT MEDICINE?

The wonders of in-vitro fertilization (IVF), or "test tube babies," have helped thousands of couples to become parents, where before they had no hope of having children. Since the first IVF birth in 1978, there are now several versions of the basic method used, suitable for different causes of infertility. They use many of the techniques and technologies of modern medicine. But some people question whether this is medicine. Does infertility constitute a disease, which causes suffering? What about breast implants and other "cosmetic" procedures? How far should the body be manipulated, because technology has now made it possible? People have different views.

Button to move blades

Handle

French tonsil guillotine *c.* 1850s

SURGICAL MEDICINE

Probing, cutting, slicing, removing, and repairing have been the basic methods of the surgeon for more than 6,000 years. The story of surgery is closely linked to several allied sciences. Like them, it has seen many fads and fashions, and many instruments that were once popular are no longer used. Inflamed, swollen tonsils at the back of the throat used to be treated by removing them with a tonsil guillotine. But it fell from use since it was unsafe. Nowadays tonsillectomy is not usually considered to be an appropriate treatment, and patients are left to recover by themselves.

Hollow tube to convey sounds

Doctor monitoring readout

Patient on ECG treadmill

Bell put on chest to pick up sound of breathing

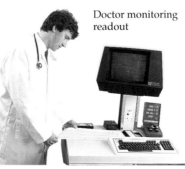

DIAGNOSTIC MEDICINE

In many Western countries, many visits to the doctor are for minor, "self-limiting" ailments – the body gets better by itself. An examination, using an instrument such as the stethoscope, helps diagnosis and rules out more serious problems. Medicine, and diagnosis in particular, have been called an art as well as a science. The doctor must be alert to not-so-medical problems, such as stress or loneliness, which may underlie the physical complaint.

SCIENCE AND MEDICINE

Advances in science and technology have made possible the development of sophisticated machines for both diagnosis and treatment. The electrocardiograph (ECG) treadmill, for example, monitors the efficiency and functioning of the heart. It is used in diagnostic medicine to indicate whether a patient is at risk of a heart attack by giving an idea of the heart's fitness when exercising. It is also used in sports medicine by athletes to investigate how their hearts respond to the stresses of physical activity.

In the beginning

ALTHOUGH THE ORIGINS of medicine are lost in the mists of time, archaeological evidence reveals that Stone Age people were familiar with healing herbs and other plants, and could also set fractured or broken bones. In ancient Egypt and Mesopotamia, complex medicine was practiced, intertwined with religion and magic. By 2000 BC Egyptian medicine had three main branches: physicians used drugs, ointments, and potions; surgeons treated injuries and the body surface, but rarely internal organs; and sorcerer-priests dealt with evil spirits and the supernatural. A handful of Egyptian documents describes drugs used for specific illnesses, made up of plants such as beans, leeks, figs, and dates, minerals like copper and antimony, and animal products ranging from hippopotamus fat to ox excrement. The first known physician was an Egyptian, Imhotep (2686-c. 2613 BC). In Mesopotamia, the Sumerians, Amorites, Babylonians, and Assyrians in turn developed their medicine. They carried out surgery, washed and bandaged wounds, and used hundreds of remedies ranging from prunes to lizard droppings. As in Egypt, specific remedies were linked to certain diseases, and medicine was combined with chants and spells.

Catnip
Nepeta cataria

Rue
Ruta graveolens

HEALING PLANTS
Archaeological evidence from preserved pollen grains shows that plants with known healing powers have been associated with human dwellings and burial sites for more than 50,000 years. Catnip was valued for its settling effects on the digestive system, and rue for its sedative properties and as a healing poultice for ulcers (although large doses can be fatal).

DEER DOCTOR
This restored version of a cave painting in Ariège, France shows a human figure adorned with deer skin and antlers. It is about 20,000 years old and may depict a healing priest, dancing to drive away evil and illness.

SURGICAL KNIVES
Very few surgical tools remain from ancient Egypt and Mesopotamia, although stone pictures as early as 3000 BC show knives, forceps, probes, and cautery irons (p. 22). In Babylonia, physicians probably removed eyelid cysts, and cut blood vessels, a common treatment over the ages. Egyptian writings describe conditions needing surgery, such as circumcision, cutting out abscesses or cysts, and lancing boils, although internal surgery was not common. Knives like these may have been used to remove organs for mummification.

Holes in the head

Preserved skulls provide hard evidence of trephining, the ancient practice of cutting holes in the skull. This may have been intended to release – from the brain or mind – the evil spirits and demons believed to cause mental problems or illnesses, such as migraine or epilepsy. In Europe, trephining continued into the 16th century. It was also practiced in North Africa, parts of Asia, New Zealand, some Pacific Islands, and South America.

Wooden bow

BOW FOR TREPHINING
Of the various trephining devices, one of the most common was the bow and drill. The bow was made of springy wood and had a leather thong wound around the drill several times. To perform the procedure, the operator positioned the drill tip on the head, steadied the other end, and "sawed" the bow back and forth, spinning the drill one way and then the other as it bored into the bone.

Leather thong

Hardwood bow shaft

Detail of reconstruction of bow end

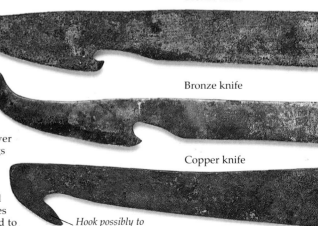

Bronze knife

Bronze knife

Copper knife

Hook possibly to ease organs out of the body

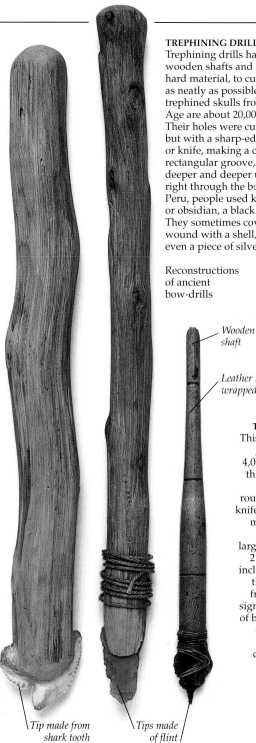

TREPHINING DRILLS

Trephining drills have smooth wooden shafts and tips of very hard material, to cut into the bone as neatly as possible. The earliest trephined skulls from the Stone Age are about 20,000 years old. Their holes were cut not by a drill but with a sharp-edged flint scraper or knife, making a circular or rectangular groove, which became deeper and deeper until it passed right through the bone. In ancient Peru, people used knives of bronze or obsidian, a black glassy rock. They sometimes covered the wound with a shell, a gourd, or even a piece of silver or gold.

Reconstructions of ancient bow-drills

Holes in head

Natural joint between skull bones

Healed bone edges from an earlier operation

Wooden shaft

Leather thong wrapped around here

TREPHINED SKULL

This skull comes from Jericho and is over 4,000 years old. It has three trephined holes. Drilled holes were roughly circular, whereas knife-cut ones were usually more square. A few skulls have up to five holes – the largest ones measuring more than 2 in (5 cm) across. Some people, including this individual, survived the process – this can be deduced from the fact that the bone shows signs of healing. In Europe, the piece of bone cut away by the knife method could be worn on a necklace cord as an amulet to ward off evil. Trephining continues today – for brain surgery in the modern operating room, using precision electric-powered drills and saws (p. 47).

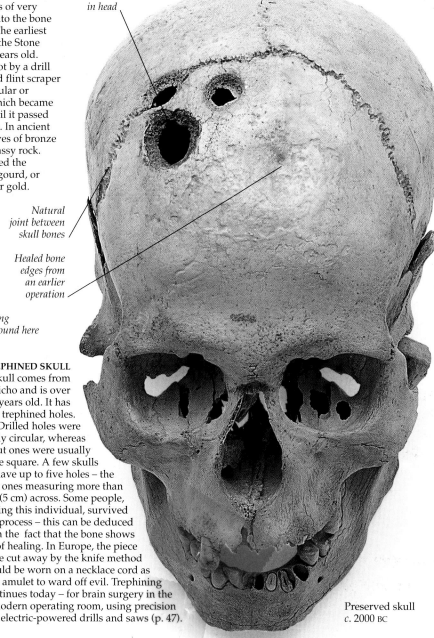

Preserved skull c. 2000 BC

Tip made from shark tooth

Tips made of flint

ASSYRIAN STONE

This is the second tablet of a medical treatise called *"If a man has a cough . . . ."* It comes from Nineveh and dates from about 700 BC. The treatise details several stomach disorders and recommends various medical remedies. Healing was practiced by priests who learned their trade from thousands of inscribed clay tablets in the city's library of Ashurbanipal, named after the Assyrian ruler (668-627 BC).

CODE OF HAMMURABI

King Hammurabi, ruler of Babylonia between 1792 and 1750 BC, established a set of laws called the Code, which have been preserved on a stone slab. Seventeen laws related to medicine, including rewarding or punishing physicians for the outcome of their treatments. For example, a physician who "opened an eye abscess of a nobleman and has caused the loss of the eye" had his hand cut off.

9

Spirits and healing

IN SOME FORMS OF TRADITIONAL MEDICINE, the main healing powers lie not with remedies, such as herbs or surgery, but in people's belief in the supernatural powers of the shaman, sometimes called a medicine man or witch doctor. In societies in which illness is believed to be caused by the presence of evil spirits, the shaman communicates with the spirit world, often while in a trance or possessed state, and calls upon the spirits to leave the patient's body. Some shamans, such as medicine men of certain North American Indian groups, also have a special knowledge of herbs and minerals. Others perform general rituals, such as influencing the weather and attracting animals to hunt. Masks and other items are often used in ceremonies, and modern research shows that the shaman's appearance, dancing, chanting, and ritual actions can have powerful effects on the mind, which may bring about physical effects in the body, perhaps aiding recovery.

Figure may represent Ododua Yoruba, mother of the gods

Man represents Eshu, the god who brought the Ifa cult into the world

PURIFICATION
This wooden mask from the island of Sri Lanka in Asia is thought to represent Garayaka, the demon of purification. In Sri Lankan medicine demons are believed to upset the balance of the Ayurvedic humors (p. 14). The balance is restored in the "Tovil" ritual in which the demons are exorcised by performers wearing masks that represent them.

ANCIENT AND MODERN
Shamanistic beliefs and ceremonies continue today in many areas of Africa. According to some estimates, there are over 200,000 witch doctors, or "sangomas" as they are called locally, in South Africa alone. They learn their craft from a spiritual teacher and are asked to protect people from harm, cure poor health, and help with affairs of the heart, although treatments and practices vary across Africa. This picture shows a shaman healing ceremony held by the Bantu people in Cameroon, West Africa. These rituals are occasionally complemented by Western medical treatments such as vaccination and drug therapy.

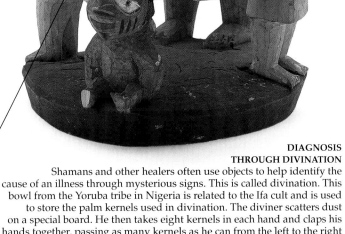

Chicken-shaped box contains palm kernels for divination

DIAGNOSIS THROUGH DIVINATION
Shamans and other healers often use objects to help identify the cause of an illness through mysterious signs. This is called divination. This bowl from the Yoruba tribe in Nigeria is related to the Ifa cult and is used to store the palm kernels used in divination. The diviner scatters dust on a special board. He then takes eight kernels in each hand and claps his hands together, passing as many kernels as he can from the left to the right hand. If one or two remain in his left hand, he makes marks on the board. Once there are eight marks on the board he can make an interpretation.

CEREMONIES AND HEALING
Medicines are not only used for disease or accidental injury. Australian Aboriginal groups have initiation rites, especially for young men, that may involve bloodletting, burning or scarring the body, or pulling teeth. Ointments and balms made from herbs and other substances are applied after the ceremony. This boy is undergoing an open, or not secret, part of an initiation rite.

*Hair secured
by rush ties*

*Eye holes allow
wearer to observe
the scene*

ADORNMENTS
Amulets and other body
adornments are believed to
have traditional magical
powers, and are intended
to protect the wearer
from evil and illness.
This amuletic necklace,
thought to have
belonged to a medicine
man from the Apache
group of North
American Indians, is
made of glass beads
and human teeth.

*Teeth still
in upper
jaw bone*

MASKS
Masks are
often used in
ceremonies and
can inspire fear as
well as belief. This
mask was worn by the medicine man of the
Iroquois Indians in North America, and probably
represents a harmful spirit that causes illness.
Shamanistic societies are traditional in parts of
the Americas, Africa, and Southeast Asia.
Shamans usually hold power in their
communities because they have
the power to communicate
with the spirits.

GOING AND GONE
Around the world, shamanistic traditions
are disappearing or already lost. American
artist-author George Catlin (1796-1872)
spent many years recording the clothes,
equipment, and customs of North American
Indian peoples, such as this Blackfoot healer
from the Montana region in the 1830s.

POINTING BONES
These pointing bones were
used by Aboriginals to cause death.
Someone wishing to kill an enemy (known as
a *Kurdaitcha*, or executioner who acquires magical powers while
seeking vengeance) builds a fire secretly and passes the bones through
the flames while uttering ritual curses. The bones are buried so the magic matures.
Later they are dug up and pointed at the sleeping enemy.

*Carved limb bone,
possibly from a kangaroo*

*Bone attached
with plant resin*

*Braided
human hair*

Plants and healing

Using plants for treating illness is probably the oldest form of medicine. Following their instincts, or perhaps by observing sick animals eat vegetation, early people may have experimented with plants, learning by trial and error. The earliest medical texts, from Egypt, Babylonia, and China, list hundreds of plant remedies. But, in reality, the choice was limited. Some plants were rare or had a short growing season. For others, only certain parts were effective, such as the young leaves or fresh roots. Not all were effective after drying and powdering. Plant remedies could be cooked or eaten fresh, drunk as a tea, inhaled as a vapor, applied to the skin as an ointment or poultice, or used as a suppository. Modern analysis shows that many ancient plant remedies contain medically active substances, and plants remain a major source of drugs (pp. 40-41).

KOLA NUTS
Kola nuts originate in West Africa. They are widely used in Africa, Asia, and South America to improve appetite and counter tiredness. They are usually chewed whole or powdered to make a tea. Kola nuts contain caffeine, the stimulant in coffee.

NATURAL NEEDLES
Plants can have both drug-related and physical uses. In some Australian Aboriginal and African cultures, sharp thorns like these from Kenya were used to sew up wounds, with threads of vine or creeper jammed into a split at the wider end. Some thorns could be made even harder if placed in the embers of a fire. This also killed the germs on them.

Black cohosh
Cimicifuga racemosa

Dried
root

MULTIPURPOSE PLANT
Black cohosh, also called squawroot, is a traditional remedy of some North American Indian tribes. It eases pain, especially nerve and muscle pain, arthritis, and headaches. It helps cramps and other muscle spasms, asthma, and reduces swelling and soreness in ailments such as coughs and sore throats. It was brought to Europe in the 19th century and is now an important part of the medical herbalist's natural pharmacy. Most preparations use the dried roots and underground stems.

WITCH HAZEL
The bushy witch hazel plant has been used by North American Indians for centuries to promote the healing of bleeding, bruises, and burns. From the 18th century its use spread into Europe and other places. Extracts of the leaves and bark are now used in commercial creams and ointments for bruises, varicose veins, and hemorrhoids (piles). Witch hazel is an astringent, causing tissues to contract and to stop bleeding as they dry out.

Witch hazel
Hamamelis virginiana

Dried leaves and bark

MEDICINE BAG
This buckskin bag was used by a medicine man (pp. 10-11) of the Plains Indians from North America between about 1880 and 1920. He would gather herbs on his travels, and even the simple action of taking remedies out of the bag would be part of the healing ritual.

NATURAL DRESSINGS
Absorbent leaves and mosses were used from prehistoric times to cover wounds and make poultices. The poultice was mixed with or soaked in the herbal remedy, then put on the affected part. This scene from about 1570 shows an Aztec healer, from what is now Mexico, applying a leg poultice to draw poisons and bad spirits (pp. 10-11) from the body.

Bump suggests figure has coca leaves in its mouth

CHEWING COCA
In South America, chewing coca leaves, as seen in this silver figure from Peru, is a traditional way of staving off hunger and exhaustion, and numbing pain and fatigue. The coca shrub *Erythroxylon coca* is now cultivated in Africa, Southeast Asia, and Australia for the medicinal chemicals called narcotic alkaloids found in its leaves. It is grown illegally as a source of the drug cocaine, which is also grown, processed, and prescribed under legal restrictions. The Incas also used mind-affecting drugs in medical-religious ceremonies (see below).

MAKING A CHOICE
The choice of remedy was an important part of the healing ceremony. This South American Indian pottery jar depicts a medicine man from the Mochica culture examining his patient before selecting plants for treatment. Often the healer or shaman carefully guarded the identity of medicinal plants and the ways in which they were prepared and prescribed, since this knowledge contributed to his status and power in the village.

Mescal or peyote
Lophophora williamsii

Eucalyptus
Eucalyptus globulus

ENDLESS USES
Eucalyptus (gum) leaves are a traditional remedy of the Australian Aboriginal people. They are used to treat fever; the vapors of crushed leaves are inhaled to clear the nose, throat, and lungs when clogged with mucus from respiratory infection; they are used to make antiseptic poultices for wounds or inflammations; and they are also made into various decoctions (boiled-down extracts) to be taken internally. Eucalyptus trees were introduced into the West in the 19th century. Russian research suggests that some species are effective against influenza viruses and malaria (p. 63), while others are active against bacteria.

SHAMAN DRUGS
Plants with hallucinogenic qualities are often used in healing ceremonies by shamans and other medicine men. In a trancelike state from the effects of the plant, the shaman is believed to be able to communicate with the gods and spirits who are either responsible for causing the illness or can help to cure it. This spineless cactus, commonly called mescal or peyote, grows in Mexico and the southwestern US. It is the source of mescaline, a mind-altering drug that was used by some North American Indians and the Aztecs. Possession of the plant is now illegal in many countries.

Eastern philosophies

IN THE EAST, MEDICAL THINKING and practice have a long and sophisticated history. Although often represented as timeless and unchanging, plenty of evidence shows the incorporation of new ideas and the abandonment of old ones. India's medical system, *Ayurveda*, meaning "knowledge of life," began about 2,400 years ago and reached its basic present form by AD 500. It is based mainly on the *Caraka samhita* and *Susruta samhita* texts, traditionally ascribed to the physician Caraka (*c.* 1000 BC) and the surgeon Susruta (possibly AD 50 or 450). In Ayurvedic medicine, illness is seen as an imbalance of the body's three main humors – bile, phlegm, and wind. They are treated with herbs, minerals, operations, ritual chants, and offerings. To the east in China, medicine was mixed with religion until AD 500, when professional doctors took over. Surgery was rare, but there were thousands of other remedies. China's key text, the *Huang Ti Nei Ching*, is traditionally ascribed to the mythical emperor Huang Ti.

TIBETAN MEDICINE
In Tibet, medicine has elements familar from China (herbal cures), Greece-Arabia (the humors of the body), and India (placing the soul in the spine). It also uses chants from Lamaism, a form of Buddhism. This traveling doctor's bag contains minerals and herbs, a horn and spatula for mixing, and a blade and sharpening stone for simple surgery.

Licorice root

Asafetida resin

Rauwolfia root

Honey

Rock salt

Myrrh gum

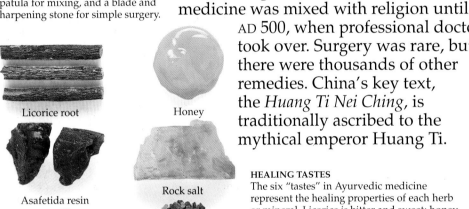

HEALING TASTES
The six "tastes" in Ayurvedic medicine represent the healing properties of each herb or mineral. Licorice is bitter and sweet; honey is sweet and astringent; asafetida resin from giant fennel is pungent; rock salt is salty; rauwolfia root is bitter (good for anxiety, headaches, and snake bites); myrrh gum is both bitter and pungent. The sixth taste, sour, comes from fruit. Medicines are applied as poultices, pastes, tablets, enemas, or bath oils.

Position for focusing chakras

THE CHAKRAS
Indian lore identifies seven chakras as centers for focusing and distributing the body's spiritual power. They are situateded along the spinal column from the top of the head to the base of the spine. Each chakra is linked to specific glands and body organs. If the chakras are unbalanced or damaged, illness results. Medicines, massage, yoga, and chants rebalance the chakras and restore health.

Probes and needles

Eye for thread based on animal gut or plant material

Blade with half-round end

Blade

Probe with blade at right angles

Blade

Secondary blade

Knife with right-angled secondary blade

THE POCKET SURGERY
Nowhere in the ancient world was surgery as sophisticated as in India. Amputation punishments for various crimes meant surgeons gained practice in cosmetic surgery as well as in sewing wounds, removing kidney and bladder stones, and many other operations. For internal surgery, black ants, which secrete an acid with strong antiseptic qualities, were used as clips instead of stitches. This 19th-century case contains instruments used for bloodletting and suturing (stitching) wounds.

Wooden case with two hinged lids

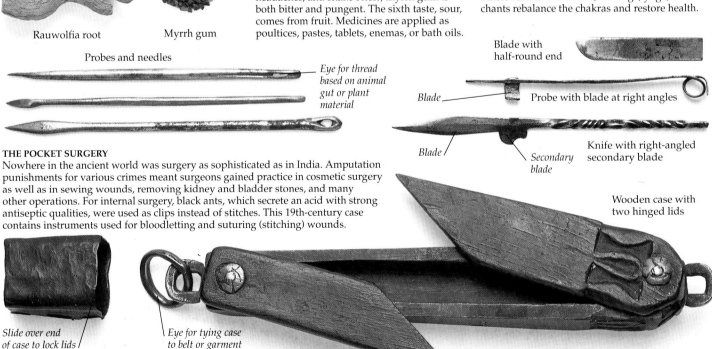

Slide over end of case to lock lids

Eye for tying case to belt or garment

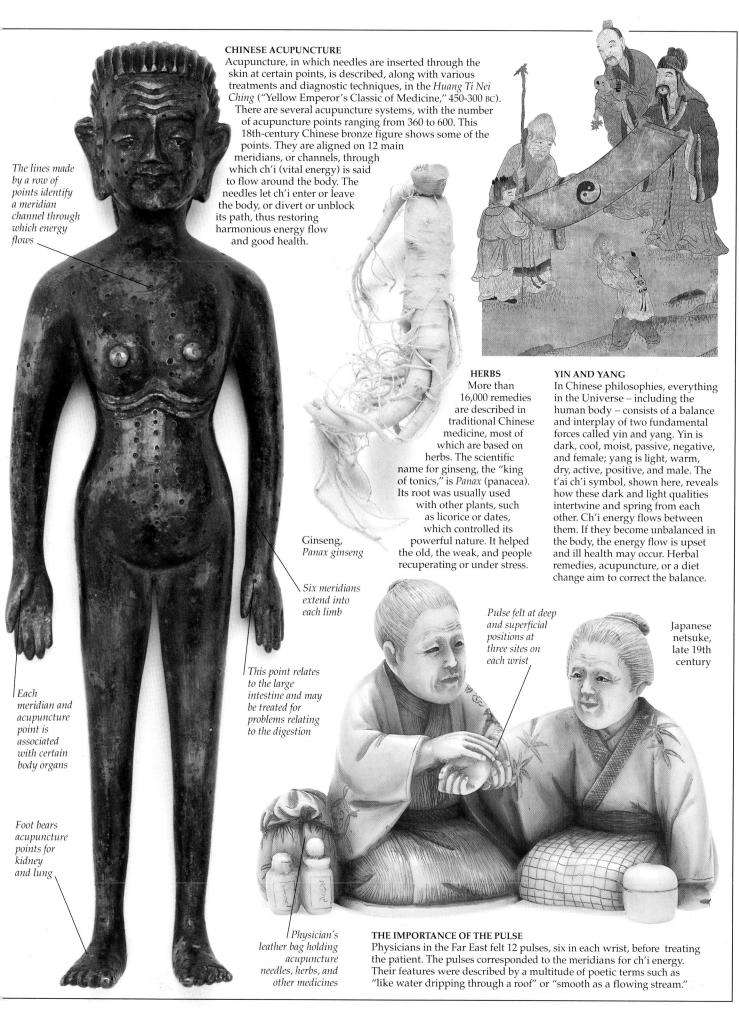

CHINESE ACUPUNCTURE
Acupuncture, in which needles are inserted through the skin at certain points, is described, along with various treatments and diagnostic techniques, in the *Huang Ti Nei Ching* ("Yellow Emperor's Classic of Medicine," 450-300 BC). There are several acupuncture systems, with the number of acupuncture points ranging from 360 to 600. This 18th-century Chinese bronze figure shows some of the points. They are aligned on 12 main meridians, or channels, through which ch'i (vital energy) is said to flow around the body. The needles let ch'i enter or leave the body, or divert or unblock its path, thus restoring harmonious energy flow and good health.

The lines made by a row of points identify a meridian channel through which energy flows

HERBS
More than 16,000 remedies are described in traditional Chinese medicine, most of which are based on herbs. The scientific name for ginseng, the "king of tonics," is *Panax* (panacea). Its root was usually used with other plants, such as licorice or dates, which controlled its powerful nature. It helped the old, the weak, and people recuperating or under stress.

Ginseng, Panax ginseng

YIN AND YANG
In Chinese philosophies, everything in the Universe – including the human body – consists of a balance and interplay of two fundamental forces called yin and yang. Yin is dark, cool, moist, passive, negative, and female; yang is light, warm, dry, active, positive, and male. The t'ai ch'i symbol, shown here, reveals how these dark and light qualities intertwine and spring from each other. Ch'i energy flows between them. If they become unbalanced in the body, the energy flow is upset and ill health may occur. Herbal remedies, acupuncture, or a diet change aim to correct the balance.

Six meridians extend into each limb

This point relates to the large intestine and may be treated for problems relating to the digestion

Pulse felt at deep and superficial positions at three sites on each wrist

Japanese netsuke, late 19th century

Each meridian and acupuncture point is associated with certain body organs

Foot bears acupuncture points for kidney and lung

Physician's leather bag holding acupuncture needles, herbs, and other medicines

THE IMPORTANCE OF THE PULSE
Physicians in the Far East felt 12 pulses, six in each wrist, before treating the patient. The pulses corresponded to the meridians for ch'i energy. Their features were described by a multitude of poetic terms such as "like water dripping through a roof" or "smooth as a flowing stream."

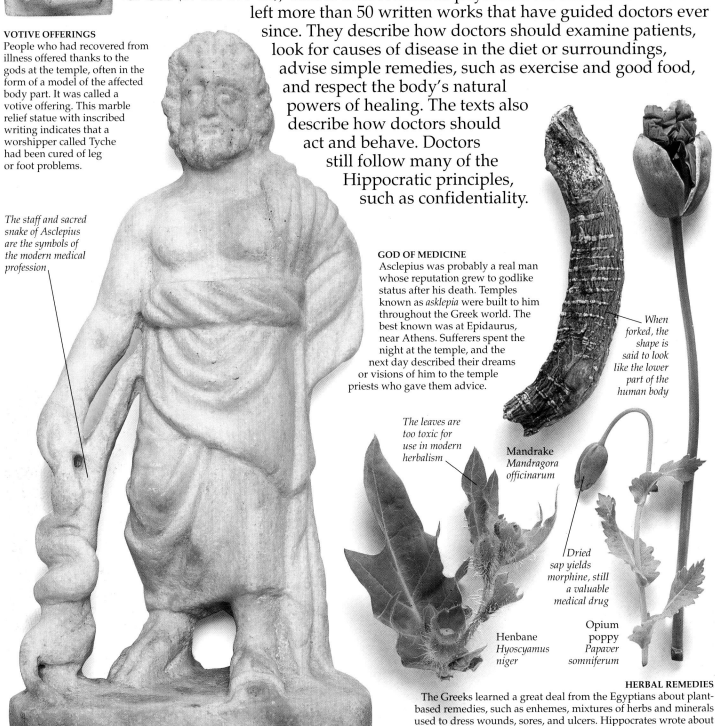

Ancient Greece

MUCH OF WESTERN SCIENCE HAS ITS ROOTS in ancient Greece, and medicine is no exception. Legend tells how the god Apollo invented healing, and how Chiron the centaur passed the knowledge to Asclepius, god of medicine, and his daughters Hygeia, goddess of health, and Panacea, goddess of healing. The cult of Asclepius arose in the 5th century BC, alongside the work of Hippocrates of Cos (*c*. 460-377 BC), Greece's most famous physician. He and his followers left more than 50 written works that have guided doctors ever since. They describe how doctors should examine patients, look for causes of disease in the diet or surroundings, advise simple remedies, such as exercise and good food, and respect the body's natural powers of healing. The texts also describe how doctors should act and behave. Doctors still follow many of the Hippocratic principles, such as confidentiality.

VOTIVE OFFERINGS
People who had recovered from illness offered thanks to the gods at the temple, often in the form of a model of the affected body part. It was called a votive offering. This marble relief statue with inscribed writing indicates that a worshipper called Tyche had been cured of leg or foot problems.

The staff and sacred snake of Asclepius are the symbols of the modern medical profession

GOD OF MEDICINE
Asclepius was probably a real man whose reputation grew to godlike status after his death. Temples known as *asklepia* were built to him throughout the Greek world. The best known was at Epidaurus, near Athens. Sufferers spent the night at the temple, and the next day described their dreams or visions of him to the temple priests who gave them advice.

When forked, the shape is said to look like the lower part of the human body

The leaves are too toxic for use in modern herbalism

Mandrake
Mandragora officinarum

Dried sap yields morphine, still a valuable medical drug

Henbane
Hyoscyamus niger

Opium poppy
Papaver somniferum

HERBAL REMEDIES
The Greeks learned a great deal from the Egyptians about plant-based remedies, such as enhemes, mixtures of herbs and minerals used to dress wounds, sores, and ulcers. Hippocrates wrote about many medicinal plants, including some with powerful, often dangerous sedative and painkilling effects, such as henbane, mandrake, and opium poppy, which were often used in surgery.

Hippocrates traveled widely but mainly taught at the medical school on Cos. One of his beliefs was that a doctor should make a prognosis – a prediction of the course and outcome of the illness, and the effects of treatment. Hippocrates' texts advise doctors to rely on observation and facts, not on gods and spirits. His book *Aphorisms*, probably the work of several people, contains many sayings and proverbs, such as "When sleep puts an end to delirium, it is a good sign." In this imaginary scene he talks with the later physician Galen of Pergamum (*c.* AD 130- 200, p. 18).

THE FOUR HUMORS

Greek science held that all things were made of four elements: air, water, fire, and earth. These were mirrored in the human body by the four "humors", or fluids: blood, phlegm, yellow bile, and black bile. If the humors lost their natural balance, illness resulted. Treatments included bleeding, laxatives, and regulating the diet.

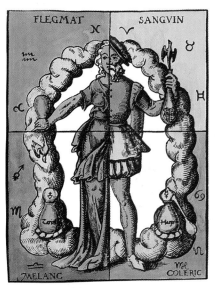

THE CONSULTATION

Most Greek doctors traveled from place to place on journeys called "epidemics." They asked patients about symptoms and examined the affected parts, using methods such as auscultation (listening, especially by pressing an ear to the body) and palpation (feeling with the fingers).

THE GREAT LIBRARY AT ALEXANDRIA

Alexander the Great founded Alexandria in Egypt in 332 BC. The city became a center of Greek learning, including medicine, and was home to a vast library. Human dissection, forbidden in Greece, allowed Herophilus (*c.* 335-280 BC) to name body parts, study the brain, and thereby begin the science of anatomy, or body structure. Erasistratus (*c.* 310-250 BC), who believed too much blood caused disease, began the science of physiology, or how the body functions.

The Roman Empire

Until Roman medicine came under the influence of the Greeks, it consisted of traditional remedies and prayers to the gods. But then in 293 BC plague swept through Rome and the Romans turned to the Greek god Asclepius (p. 16) for help. Gradually Greek doctors moved to Rome, bringing Greek ideas with them. The first physician to arrive was Asclepiades (124-c. 60 BC). Two popular Roman encyclopedic works were *De Re Medicina* ("On Medicine") by Cornelius Celsus (c. 20 BC–AD 45), mainly based on Hippocratic texts, and *Historia Naturalis* ("Natural History") by Caius Pliny the Elder (AD 23-79), which included surgery, herbs, magic, and folklore. But Claudius Galen (c. AD 130-200), anatomist, physician, and theorist was Rome's greatest medical figure. He followed Hippocrates' concept of the four humors (p. 17), but also believed in a life spirit, or *pneuma*, taken in with each breath. Along with the natural spirit from digested food, it kept the body organs active and fed. Western medicine upheld these theories for 15 centuries.

SAVING EYESIGHT
Some Roman surgeons devoted themselves solely to the removal of cataracts, opaque areas that sometimes occur in the lens of the eye, which can cause blindness. They were the first specialized eye doctors, often called oculists or ophthalmologists.

Oculist's seal found in the Moselle River, Germany

Carrying ring

Oil flask

Handle of strigil

FALSE TEETH
The earliest false teeth were made in Egypt 4,500 years ago. Roman dentists made bridges (tooth-holders) of gold, to hold extracted teeth without roots, or false teeth of ivory or metal. They also recommended toothpastes made from all manner of ingredients, including one from honey, salt, vinegar, and ground-up glass.

Replicas of Roman false teeth

PUBLIC HEALTH
The Romans knew disease was linked to dirty water, human waste, and even marshy areas. So clean water was available in private and public places for bathing, drinking, cooking, and flushing latrines, such as these at Ostia, close to Rome. Marcus Varro (116-27 BC) anticipated the germ theory (p. 32) when he said that it was unhealthy to live by a marsh since "there are bred . . . minute creatures which cannot be seen . . . which . . . enter the body through the mouth and nose and there cause serious disease."

BATHING
In the time of Imperial Rome (between the 1st century BC and the 5th century AD), a visit to the communal bath (hot or cold) could be a social occasion, or for personal hygiene, or as medical treatment advised by the physician. The skin was anointed with oil from a flask, and then rubbed with scraperlike devices called strigils to remove sweat, dirt, and small animal pests, such as lice. The hair was also kept trimmed and washed.

Curved metal blade of strigil scrapes skin

DRAWING OUT BAD HUMORS

Cupping was a popular Roman practice that aimed to draw poisonous substances and "vicious humors" from the body. A cup containing a piece of burning cloth was pressed on the skin. The burning used up the oxygen in the air in the cup, producing a partial vacuum, which powerfully sucked the cup onto the body. Dry cupping was performed on unbroken skin; wet cupping covered a wound or deliberate incision, and drew out blood, pus, and other fluids.

Bronze cupping vessel excavated from Pompeii (preserved AD 79)

Cupping vessel clamped to skin

Burning cloth in cupping vessel

Blister caused by suction

Dry cupping

ROMAN HERBS

Most Roman physicians prescribed only rest, bathing, a change of diet, and herbal remedies. There were hundreds of herbal remedies (though fewer than, for example, their Chinese contemporaries). Military physician Pedanius Dioscorides (AD 41-68), who served under the Emperor Nero (AD 37-68), compiled the first thorough *Materia Medica*, or catalog of herbs (p. 40). Today, we would regard about one-fifth of them as truly medicinal. Dioscorides followed Hippocrates (pp. 16-17) in recommending fennel to promote breast milk production in new mothers.

Fennel
Foeniculum vulgare

FISHY TREATMENTS

More than 2,000 years before ECT (p. 46), the electric ray or torpedo fish provided the first electrotherapy. Rays were kept in seawater tanks. The patient might have been immersed and suffered the ray's 500-volt shocks through the water. This may have been used to treat joint and muscle pain or paralysis.

Torpedo fish
Torpedo nobiliana

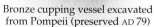

Fine-toothed bone saw for amputations

Wooden handle of saw has not been preserved

Sharp edge of blade is protected in handle

Folding knife

Traction hook for holding muscles and blood vessels out of the way during surgery

Probe for exploring wounds or diseased tissues

Fine forceps for removing splinters

ROMAN SURGICAL TOOLS

Archaeological finds have revealed thousands of Roman instruments, many of durable, well-finished bronze. Some hardly differ from modern equivalents (pp. 50-51). As well as probes, hooks, and forceps, they include various specula – devices with hinged spatula-like blades – which were inserted into an orifice and separated, to allow examination inside the body. The Greek physician and surgeon, Soranus (AD 98-138), living in the Roman Empire, wrote about using specula to investigate and diagnose female conditions.

BATTLEFIELD MEDICINE

The expansion of the Roman Empire led to many battles and many wounded. Julius Caesar (c. 100-44 BC) introduced the idea of physicians on the battlefield – the first army medical officers, who could give on-the-spot first aid at advanced "dressing stations."
The injured were sent to hospital-like *valetudinaria*, perhaps influenced by the *asklepia* (p. 16) of Greece, to recover. Similar institutions were built for Imperial officers, and then wealthy citizens, and even slaves. Gradually public hospitals evolved.

The Islamic tradition

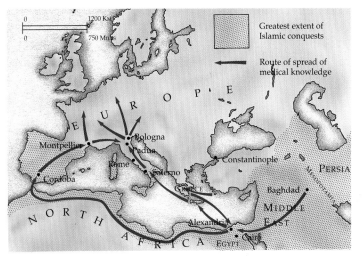

MAGIC-MEDICINAL BOWL
This Syrio-Egyptian bowl dates from the mid-13th century. It was used to cure various conditions and has been well used. The inscription reads: "This blessed cup neutralizes all poisons. In it have been gathered proven benefits . . . It is useful for the bite of serpent and scorpion . . . for abdominal pain . . . for all diseases and afflictions. The afflicted person or his agent drinks from it and then they will be cured, by the help of God."

By ABOUT THE 5TH CENTURY AD, the Roman Empire had declined and Europe was descending into the Dark Ages. Much Greek and Roman medical knowledge was lost as physicians turned to superstition and religion. But Greco-Roman traditions were maintained farther to the south and east. In AD 431 the bishop Nestorius of Constantinople was accused of heresy by the Christian Church. As a result, he and his followers fled east as far as Persia. As they traveled, they set up schools of medicine, notably in Greece, Mesopotamia, and Persia. They also translated Greek and Roman medical works into Arabic. The Byzantine Empire (the eastern half of the Roman Empire), centered on Constantinople, condemned the followers of Nestorius, but its rulers followed their example and set up centers of medical excellence and hospitals for the poor. Then from the 7th century, the followers of the prophet Mohammed, the Arabic founder of the Islamic religion, invaded Persia, the Middle East, North Africa, and parts of Spain. They adopted the translations of the Greek and Roman medical works and set up medical schools and hospitals in Baghdad (now in Iraq), Cairo in Egypt, and Cordoba in Spain.

WEST, EAST, WEST
The general body of Western medical knowledge grew with the civilizations of Egypt, Greece, and Rome. As the Roman Empire declined, this knowledge, lost in Europe, was transferred into North Africa and the Middle East. It was saved and complemented in Arabic translations, particularly in the Islamic centers of Baghdad, Cairo, and Cordoba. From the 12th century, European scholars began to translate the Arabic works back into Latin, and the ancient medical knowledge returned to Europe.

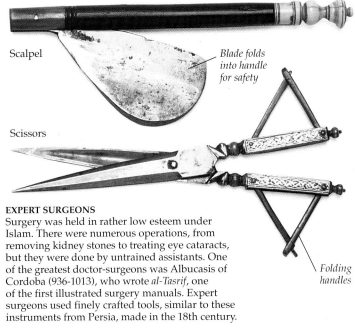

Scalpel

Blade folds into handle for safety

Scissors

Folding handles

EXPERT SURGEONS
Surgery was held in rather low esteem under Islam. There were numerous operations, from removing kidney stones to treating eye cataracts, but they were done by untrained assistants. One of the greatest doctor-surgeons was Albucasis of Cordoba (936-1013), who wrote *al-Tasrif*, one of the first illustrated surgery manuals. Expert surgeons used finely crafted tools, similar to these instruments from Persia, made in the 18th century.

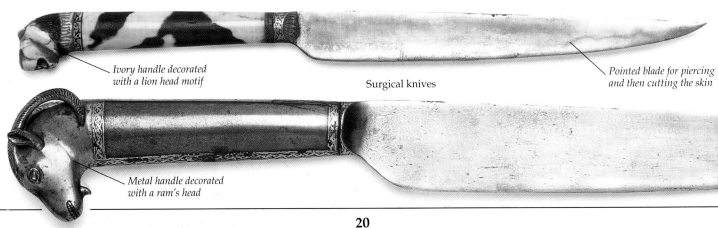

Ivory handle decorated with a lion head motif

Surgical knives

Pointed blade for piercing and then cutting the skin

Metal handle decorated with a ram's head

Rhazes

Avicenna

ISLAMIC WRITERS

Rhazes (*c.* 850-932) practiced medicine in Persia and Baghdad. The first to distinguish between smallpox and measles, he generally recommended simple treatments, such as nutritious food, rather than complex drugs. He wrote over 230 medical works. Avicenna of Persia (980-1037) was probably the most influential Islamic physician. His book *Canon of Medicine* was one million words long. Later translated into Latin, it became a major work in European medical schools, rivaling Galen (p. 18).

HERBALS

This page from an 11th-century Arabic book of herbs shows agrimony, a plant used to ease sore gums and throats, stop bleeding, and treat ailments of the stomach, liver, and gallbladder. The book catalogs 600 plants and is derived from the original Greek text *De Materia Medica*, which was compiled in the 1st century AD by Pedanius Dioscorides (p. 19), an army doctor, who studied the plants of many regions. Many Greek and Roman texts that would have been lost forever were preserved in Arabic translations.

Iron pestle handle

Glaze can be easily cleaned

Mortar, 18th century

Arabic date reads 1207, which is 1792 in the Western calendar

REMEDY PREPARATION

Arabic medicine was famed for its enormous natural pharmacy, including plant substances such as camphor, myrrh, senna, and cloves. One of the most common ways of preparing remedies was to crush them with a mortar and pestle, and then incorporate them into elixirs, syrups, balms, and other preparations. Raw materials were not always pounded dry – some were mashed in water, oil, or alcohol to extract the substance required.

STORING MEDICINES

Dried herbs, minerals, and other medicines were stored in pottery drug jars by the apothecary. This Persian jar was made in the 9th century. Some jars stored blood that had been let from patients, a common treatment of the time (p. 22). It was used in remedies, especially for stomach upsets. Arabic physicians also often prescribed animal products such as ambergris, a by-product from the intestines of the sperm whale.

Magic and superstition

BETWEEN THE 5TH AND 15TH CENTURIES IN EUROPE, there was little progress in the sciences, particularly in medicine. A few medical schools flourished, influenced by Islamic practice (pp. 20-21), notably at Salerno in Italy, Montpellier in France (founded *c.* 1167), and Bologna (1158) and Padua (1222), also in Italy. But everyday medicine regressed into mixtures of herbalism, magic, and religious ritual. In this early period the *pneumas* and humors of Galen (p. 18) ruled medical thought and were gradually adopted into the Christian view of disease as God's punishment for people's sins. The physical body was less important than the fate of the soul after death. Diagnosis and treatment were often based on superstitions, religious signs, and prayers to the healing saints. Some public medical care was available, provided by the Christian Church, in the hospitals run by convents, abbeys, and monasteries.

BEZOAR STONES
These natural rocklike objects form in the stomachs of animals, such as goats, sheep, and cows, and were said to have magical powers against disease-causing "poisons" in the body. Human stones from the bladder, kidney, and gall bladder were similarly prized.

Each segment is named and filled with a different herb

LET IT BLEED
The ancient practice of bloodletting or bleeding kept its popularity during the Middle Ages. The basic idea was to drain "poisons" or excess blood from the body, thereby restoring the balance of the humors (p. 17). Different illnesses had to be treated by bleeding from different places. Complex charts showed where the bleeding knife or leeches (p. 26), which removed blood more slowly than by knife, should be applied. Like cupping (p. 19), bleeding was still practiced in the 19th century.

PLAGUE AND POMANDERS
From the 1320s, the terrible Black Death swept through Mongolia and China, across Asia, and into northern Europe 20 years later. It was the bubonic plague, a bacterial infection spread by rat flea bites, which killed over 70 million Europeans. The Christian religion viewed it as God's retribution for the sins of humankind. This eight-section gold and silver pomander carried fragrant-scented petals and herbs, with the aim of freshening the air and so keeping the plague (and the stench of death) at bay.

TAKING URINE
Medieval doctors observed and interviewed their patients, and perhaps felt the pulse, but uroscopy – the examination of their urine – was most important. There were up to 30 features to note, including color, sediment, smell, and taste. These provided the basis for diagnosis, and guided treatment. In many places the urine flask became the symbol of the doctor. Uroscopy continued into the 19th century.

Sprinkler, probably for wine or holy water

Split tip for holding wafers of holy bread

Tip placed in fire to become red-hot

CAUTERY IRON (*above*)
Cautery irons were heated red-hot like branding irons, and applied to burn and seal bleeding areas, such as skin ulcers and amputation stumps. This long-handled version was used on buboes, the painful swellings in the armpits, groin, and neck that were characteristic of bubonic plague.

Palm frond

Saint Lucy's new eyes

SAINTS COSMOS AND DAMIAN
Two famous healing saints were the twin brothers Cosmos and Damian. Famed for their free care of the sick, they were beheaded in *c.* AD 278 by the Emperor Diocletian for refusing to give up Christianity. This painting by Jaume Huguet (1415-1492) depicts the legend of how they replaced the gangrenous leg of a sufferer with the healthy leg of a man who had just died.

Wild pansy or heartsease (Viola tricolor)

DOCTRINE OF SIGNATURES
The doctrine of signatures has existed in various forms since antiquity. If a plant was "signed" – showed features resembling symptoms of an illness, or looked like a part of the body – then it was used to cure that illness or body part. Tea made from heart-shaped wild pansy petals, for example, reputedly mended or "eased" a broken heart, hence its other name of heartsease. Similarly, the forked mandrake root (p. 16), thought to look like the lower body, was used to promote fertility.

Eyes on a platter

THE HEALING SAINTS
The medieval ill could pray and make offerings to various healing saints. This plaque is of Saint Lucy of Syracuse, who was martyred in the 3rd century AD during the persecution of the Christians by the Roman Emperor Diocletian. She became a patron of eye problems because legend told how she never wished to marry; when a suitor admired her eyes, she plucked them out in scorn to discourage his advances. Miraculously, they grew back again.

TOUCHPIECES
Some kings and rulers were believed to have healing powers, curing their subjects by touch or with gifts. These gold touchpieces from the reign of James I of England (1603-1625) were thought to cure a widespread, disfiguring form of tuberculosis (TB) called scrofula. Over 92,000 sufferers lined up for Charles II to touch them between 1661 and 1665.

CARING AT ARM'S LENGTH *(below)*
Priests helped to care for, comfort, and bless the sick. But they also kept them at arm's length, with devices such as this 16th-century long-handled communion instrument for dispensing holy bread or wine. These allowed them to avoid close contact, especially with plague sufferers and lepers.

Long, silver-plated handle

Ebony handle to insulate fingers from heat

Renaissance and revolution

From about the 14th century, a renaissance, or rebirth, of interest in the arts and sciences spread from Italy across Europe. This involved a rediscovery and also some criticism of classical learning. Galileo Galilei (1564-1642), for example, through using a telescope, pressed the argument that the Earth is not the center of the Universe. In this new spirit of inquiry, people such as Leonardo da Vinci and Andreas Vesalius began to dissect human corpses, a practice that had not previously been very common, to discover the structures and workings of the body. Following pioneering work by the Italians Realdo Colombo and Andrea Cesalpino, the English physician William Harvey (1578-1657) showed that blood actively circulates throughout the body, pumped by the heart. His simple experiments contradicted the Galenic tradition of blood being produced from food and drink and consumed in the tissues. Harvey's work met with much criticism, but this scientific approach became a central feature of modern mechanical physiology (thinking of the body as a machine).

PARACELSUS
The Swiss doctor Paracelsus (1493-1541), rejected the teachings of Galen and Avicenna (p. 18 and p. 21), arguing against overcomplicated drug mixtures and operations. He was also a pioneer of using minerals, such as sulfur, lead, iron, and mercury, as drugs rather than just using plant and animal products.

Kidney

Intestines

Frontispiece of Vesalius' great work

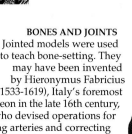

Joints corresponding to human shoulder, elbow, wrist, and so on

THE ANATOMISTS
The first great anatomical work was *De Humani Corporis Fabrica* ("Fabric of the Human Body", 1543) by Andreas Vesalius (1514-1564), professor of anatomy at Padua University. The Italian artist-scientist Leonardo da Vinci (1452-1519) had been the first to draw anatomical pictures of what he actually saw, rather than what the ancients taught, but his works were lost for over 300 years.

BONES AND JOINTS
Jointed models were used to teach bone-setting. They may have been invented by Hieronymus Fabricius (*c.* 1533-1619), Italy's foremost surgeon in the late 16th century, who devised operations for tying arteries and correcting spinal deformities.

TEACHING ANATOMY
Some religious restrictions on dissection were lifted in the 15th century, leading to the wider study of anatomy using models like these as extra teaching aids. But although some progress was made, ideas about the causes of disease continued to be based on the theories of Hippocrates and Galen (p. 16 and p. 18), and common medical practice hardly changed at all.

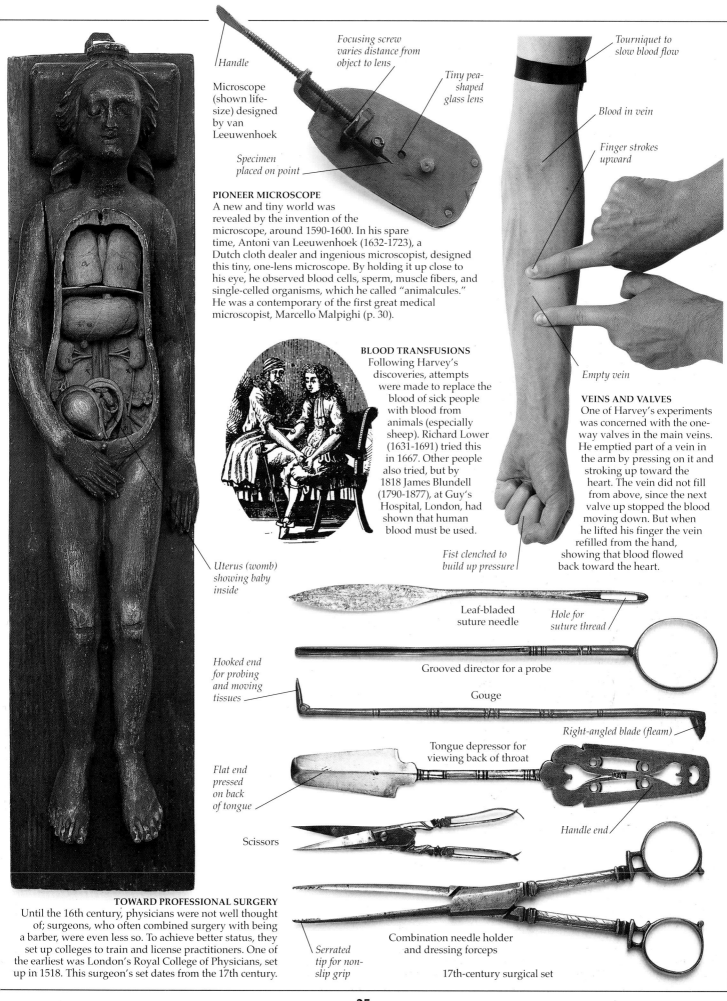

Handle

Focusing screw varies distance from object to lens

Tiny pea-shaped glass lens

Microscope (shown life-size) designed by van Leeuwenhoek

Specimen placed on point

PIONEER MICROSCOPE
A new and tiny world was revealed by the invention of the microscope, around 1590-1600. In his spare time, Antoni van Leeuwenhoek (1632-1723), a Dutch cloth dealer and ingenious microscopist, designed this tiny, one-lens microscope. By holding it up close to his eye, he observed blood cells, sperm, muscle fibers, and single-celled organisms, which he called "animalcules." He was a contemporary of the first great medical microscopist, Marcello Malpighi (p. 30).

BLOOD TRANSFUSIONS
Following Harvey's discoveries, attempts were made to replace the blood of sick people with blood from animals (especially sheep). Richard Lower (1631-1691) tried this in 1667. Other people also tried, but by 1818 James Blundell (1790-1877), at Guy's Hospital, London, had shown that human blood must be used.

Tourniquet to slow blood flow

Blood in vein

Finger strokes upward

Empty vein

VEINS AND VALVES
One of Harvey's experiments was concerned with the one-way valves in the main veins. He emptied part of a vein in the arm by pressing on it and stroking up toward the heart. The vein did not fill from above, since the next valve up stopped the blood moving down. But when he lifted his finger the vein refilled from the hand, showing that blood flowed back toward the heart.

Fist clenched to build up pressure

Uterus (womb) showing baby inside

Hooked end for probing and moving tissues

Leaf-bladed suture needle

Hole for suture thread

Grooved director for a probe

Gouge

Right-angled blade (fleam)

Flat end pressed on back of tongue

Tongue depressor for viewing back of throat

Handle end

Scissors

TOWARD PROFESSIONAL SURGERY
Until the 16th century, physicians were not well thought of; surgeons, who often combined surgery with being a barber, were even less so. To achieve better status, they set up colleges to train and license practitioners. One of the earliest was London's Royal College of Physicians, set up in 1518. This surgeon's set dates from the 17th century.

Serrated tip for non-slip grip

Combination needle holder and dressing forceps

17th-century surgical set

Progress and practice

THE SPIRIT OF RESEARCH and experimentation begun in the Renaissance (pp. 24-25) brought great advances in medical understanding and techniques. However, these took a very long time to filter through to the daily practices of the average physician. In Europe in the 17th century, traditional treatments, such as blood-letting by blade or leech, and cautery (burning, p. 22), were still popular for all sorts of ailments. But new ideas, such as those of Paré (p. 54) and others, gradually found their uses in everyday medicine. The English physician Thomas Sydenham (1624-1689) reminded doctors that their first priority should be to treat their patients, not test theories or prescribe increasingly complex surgery or drugs. Sydenham's ideas were admired by Hermann Boerhaave (1668-1738), a Dutch physician and professor at Leiden University. Boerhaave was partly responsible for many of today's teaching methods, such as involving students in autopsies to show the cause of death.

THE "ENGLISH HIPPOCRATES"
Thomas Sydenham established the basis for modern clinical medicine. He recommended observing and talking to the patient, using common sense, simple treatments, and studying the progress of each disease – as advised 2,000 years earlier by Hippocrates (pp. 16-17). He described diseases in detail, and prescribed Peruvian bark (quinine) for malaria.

SUCKING BLOOD
Through the ages, the leech, the blood-sucking relative of the earthworm, has been used to rid the body of what were thought to be poisoned humors (p. 18) and evil spirits. Placed on the skin, it can drink five times its own weight in blood. Chemicals in its mucus prevent the blood from clotting. Leeching was still popular in the 19th century – in 1833, in France alone, over 40 million medicinal leeches were imported.

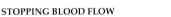

Brass screw

Clamp

Leather and metal buckle with iron teeth to grip strap

Canvas strap or belt

STOPPING BLOOD FLOW
The Petit tourniquet, named after its inventor Jean Louis Petit (1674-1750), was used in the 18th century to prevent excess bleeding during amputation. The belt was pulled tight around the limb above the wound, with the screw over the main artery. Turning the screw compressed the artery and (hopefully) some of the main nerves, helping to numb pain. Postoperative bleeding was a major problem until anesthetics (p. 48) allowed the surgeon the time to find and tie up all the blood vessels properly.

AMPUTATION SET
To prevent the galloping infection that happened after wounds and injuries, amputation was sometimes a treatment of first resort. This case of amputation instruments is more than 200 years old, and was made in Scotland. Most of the pieces are of polished wood and steel, for easy cleaning – though the role of germs and dirt in passing on infection was not understood at the time. Most surgeons saw no need to wash their hands before starting work.

Forceps

Spanner for changing saw blade

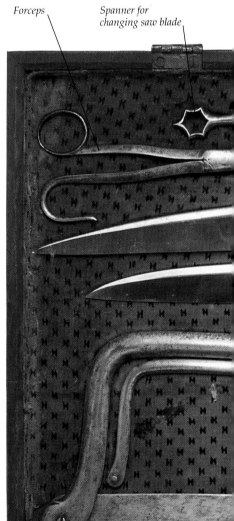

COPING WITH PAIN
Until the 19th century and the discovery of effective anesthesia, there was no medically sound way of numbing pain during surgery. Some patients drank huge quantities of alcohol while others were knocked out or fainted in agony. Most had to be held down screaming, as shown in this cartoon by William Hogarth (1697-1764). Their struggles made the surgeon's job much more difficult.

BLADDER STONE REMOVAL

The lithotome was a slim instrument inserted up the urethra, the tube from which urine flows, into the bladder. Its blade was moved to grip small bladder stones, or cut up larger ones so they could be passed out. It was a painful and dangerous operation and, without anesthetic, speed was vital. Dr. William Cheselden (1688-1752) could do it in under a minute.

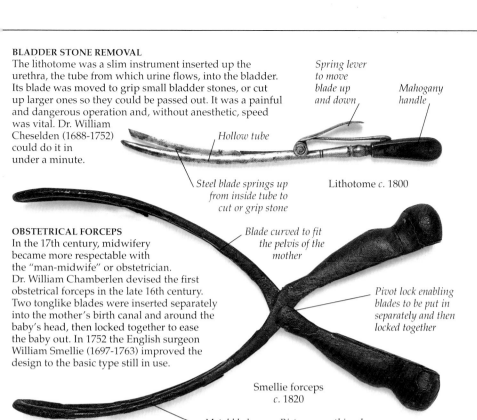

Spring lever to move blade up and down

Mahogany handle

Hollow tube

Steel blade springs up from inside tube to cut or grip stone

Lithotome *c.* 1800

Blade curved to fit the pelvis of the mother

OBSTETRICAL FORCEPS

In the 17th century, midwifery became more respectable with the "man-midwife" or obstetrician. Dr. William Chamberlen devised the first obstetrical forceps in the late 16th century. Two tonglike blades were inserted separately into the mother's birth canal and around the baby's head, then locked together to ease the baby out. In 1752 the English surgeon William Smellie (1697-1763) improved the design to the basic type still in use.

Pivot lock enabling blades to be put in separately and then locked together

Smellie forceps *c.* 1820

Metal blade covered with leather

THE HUNTERS

John Hunter (1728-1793) is regarded as one of the greatest surgeons. He was a major figure in raising surgery from its lowly beginnings, in the hands of barber-surgeons (p. 25) and quacks, to its position as a full hospital specialty. His brother William (1718-1783) was a famed physician and obstetrician. John's collection of over 13,000 anatomical specimens, both human and animal, form the basis of the Hunterian Museum at London's Royal College of Surgeons.

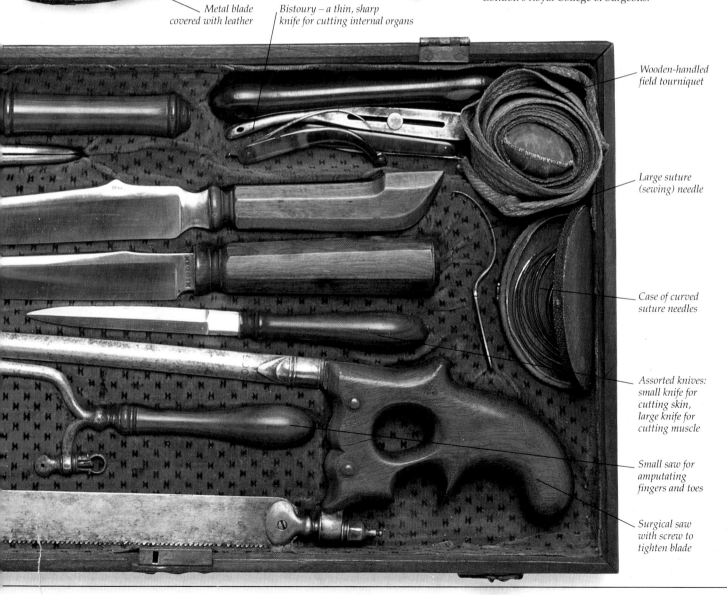

Bistoury – a thin, sharp knife for cutting internal organs

Wooden-handled field tourniquet

Large suture (sewing) needle

Case of curved suture needles

Assorted knives: small knife for cutting skin, large knife for cutting muscle

Small saw for amputating fingers and toes

Surgical saw with screw to tighten blade

Advances in diagnosis

Many medical instruments for treatment have a long history. Some of those used for examination and diagnosis are less old. As the ancient beliefs about invisible humors faded (p. 18), doctors came to believe that diseases were caused by malformation or malfunction of the body's organs or systems. They invented a whole new range of techniques and devices for clinical diagnosis – examining the patient to identify the ailment. As early as 1612 the Italian scientist Sanctorius (1561-1636) had experimented with taking body temperature. But measuring body temperature was not considered to be useful and did not come into general use until the 1880s. Likewise, other devices, such as the one-minute watch, devised in 1707 by the English physician John Floyer (1649-1734), and used for timing the pulse rate, did not gain widespread use until the 19th century. In 1781 in Vienna, Leopold Auenbrugger (1722-1809) devised percussion – tapping the chest or another body part and listening to the resonant quality of the sounds. The French doctor René Laënnec (1781-1826) devised the stethoscope and carried out clinical research linking sounds to diseases.

EYE EXAMINATION
The blood vessels and nerves inside the eye can be seen relatively easily, and their condition gives valuable information about the patient's health. In about 1850 the German scientist Hermann von Helmholtz (1821-1894), invented the reflecting ophthalmoscope for illuminating and viewing the inside of the eye. This slightly later version acts as a mirror to reflect light into the eye, with a central peephole for viewing.

Peep-hole

Handle

Endoscope is turned over so candle flame is under funnel

Candle is lit first

Funnel

Cone-shaped speculum is placed in patient's ear

Eyepiece with magnifying lens

Extra eyepiece allows an instant second opinion

LOOKING INSIDE
An endoscope (pp. 52-53) is an instrument for looking inside the body through an orifice (opening) or incision. There are many specialized designs, such as the bronchoscope for the lung airways, cystoscope for the bladder, gastroscope for the stomach, and proctoscope for the rectum. Since it is dark inside the body, the endoscope needs a light source. This 1880s otoscope, for peering into the ear, uses a candle.

Aneroid barometer dial shows change in blood pressure

Pressure-release screw

BLOOD PRESSURE
The sphygmomanometer measures blood pressure, an indicator of circulatory health. This early example (1883), unlike modern ones (p. 61), has no cuff, and the U-tube is replaced by a barometer-like aneroid device. To take the maximum blood pressure, a pelotte, or bulb, is pressed on the wrist radial artery until the pulse cannot be felt.

Pelotte is pressed onto radial artery in the arm, until the pulse disappears

CLINICAL DIAGNOSIS
Clinical medicine deals directly with the patient – questioning, observing, examining, and taking X-rays, rather than laboratory analysis and other tests. (In practice, a clinical examination usually suggests a diagnosis, which is confirmed by tests.) During the 18th and 19th centuries rival schools of clinical medicine, with different theories and emphases on disease, arose in most European cities, especially Edinburgh, Vienna, Paris, Dublin, and London. These medical students are receiving clinical instruction in a Russian hospital, around 1900.

PULSE RATE

One of the doctor's first diagnostic tests is to feel the "quality" of the pulse and count its rate. Floyer's "Physician's pulse watch" of 1707 ran for exactly one minute, but it had little success until the 19th century, when pulse rate and quality were recognized as important. Here, Elizabeth Garrett (later Garrett Anderson, 1837-1917), Britain's first woman doctor, is using a watch to take a pulse. Her long campaigns did much to remove prejudice and legal constraints against women becoming physicians.

Brass case wick-burner to heat urine

Leather case

Heatproof sample tube

Urinometer in silk bag

Litmus papers for testing acidity

Sample jar

MEASURING BREATHING

The vital capacity of the lungs – the largest amount of air they can hold – indicates the health of the respiratory system, and can be measured with a spirometer. The patient's breath bubbles up into a water-filled collecting drum underneath and raises an upturned cylinder. The spirometer was developed in England in the 1840s. This French iron-and-brass model dates from the late 19th century. Modern versions are useful in diagnosing lung conditions, such as asthma and emphysema.

Measuring scale

Incoming breath pushes up sliding cylinder inside

Water-filled drum

Patient breathes into tube connected here

URINALYSIS

By the 19th century, uroscopy (p. 22) was giving way to urinalysis – the analysis, often chemical, of the dozens of substances in urine, such as the sugar that may indicate diabetes. The chemical profile of urine can help diagnose numerous illnesses of the blood, kidneys, digestive system, and hormonal glands. This urine test kit includes a urinometer, which measures the specific gravity, or density, of urine. This can be used in the diagnosis of diabetes.

Earpiece for physician

Laënnec-type stethoscope c. 1820

BODY SOUNDS

Body sounds, such as breathing, heartbeat, and intestinal gurgles, can indicate health or disease. Until the 19th century a few physicians practiced immediate auscultation – pressing their ear to the patient's body. Then in 1816 René Laënnac invented the monaural (one-ear) stethoscope, which made the sounds clearer (and caused less embarrassment). His book, *On Mediate Auscultation*, published in 1819, included a free gift of a stethoscope from the author. The binaural (two-ear) stethoscope (p. 7), developed in the 1850s, is still one of a doctor's essential tools.

Counterbalance weight

Wooden tube-shaped body

Large chestpiece, put on patient to listen to the lungs, can be replaced with smaller one for listening to the heart

Wooden handle

Percussor

Pleximeter

Ivory plate of pleximeter bears measuring scale

Metal head with rubber tip

PERCUSSION

Auenbrugger devised medical percussion from the practice of tapping wine casks to assess their contents. When tapped, a healthy chest produces a hollow sound, but fluid or certain diseases change this to a dull, flat thud. The pleximeter, invented in the early 19th century, was held on the skin and tapped with the hammer. Some thought this gave clearer sounds than just using the fingers.

Beyond the human eye

FROM THE MID-17TH CENTURY the microscope revealed a whole new world of tissues and cells. Medical researchers began to describe and name these microscopic structures. In Bologna, Marcello Malpighi (1628-1694) studied microanatomy in animals and humans. He described the tiny blood vessels called capillaries, which link arteries to veins, thereby completing the route for the circulation of blood that had been suggested by Harvey (p. 25). German scientist-philosopher Johannes Müller (1801-1858), one of the greatest physiologists (someone who studies how the body functions), pioneered the microscopic study of diseased tissues and cells, which is called cellular pathology. His pupil Theodor Schwann (1810-1882) developed the now-familiar idea of the cell as the basic unit of life, with all living things made from cells. Another pupil, Jakob Henle (1809-1885), wrote the first textbook of anatomy to describe cells and tissues as well as larger parts. Rudolf Virchow, another student of Müller, became the first professor of pathology at Berlin, and is recognized as the founder of cellular pathology.

"ALL CELLS COME FROM CELLS"
Rudolf Virchow (1821-1902) studied leukemia and blood clotting. He adapted Schwann's cell theory to include the newly observed process of cell division, and stated that "All cells come from cells." His great work *Cellular Pathology* (1858) helped to bury the old humoral theory (p. 18). It showed that many diseases can be diagnosed and explained at the cellular level, and opened the way for scientific studies of pathology.

Eyepiece lenses

Inner barrel slides inside outer barrel

Focusing rack moves inner barrel

Outer barrel

Focusing wheel

Telescopic stand to adjust angle of main barrels

THE MICROSCOPE
This classic monocular (one-eye) compound (several-lens) microscope has many features still present today. The specimen is illuminated with light from below, which shines through it, up toward the eye. The objective lens, just above the specimen on the stage, could be changed for different magnifications. The eminent English microscopist Joseph Jackson Lister (1786-1869) calculated the curvature of the magnifying lenses to reduce chromatic aberration, a problem where colored fringes appear around objects. This 1826 model of his was the first to have such lenses. (His son was Joseph Lister, p. 48.)

THIN SLICES
Valentin knives were used to cut very thin slices of tissue for microscopic examination. They were named after Gabriel Gustav Valentin (1810-1883) of Bern, who by 1838 had observed the process of cell division, thereby helping to advance the cell theory. In 1841 he was the first to observe one type of the microorganism *Trypanosoma*, now known to cause sleeping sickness.

Slice of tissue comes out here

Double blades

Sliding adjuster

Conveyor belt to carry away slices

Caldwell automatic microtome *c.* 1884

Flywheel for smooth operation

Specimen block placed here

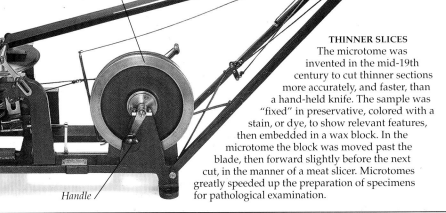

THINNER SLICES
The microtome was invented in the mid-19th century to cut thinner sections more accurately, and faster, than a hand-held knife. The sample was "fixed" in preservative, colored with a stain, or dye, to show relevant features, then embedded in a wax block. In the microtome the block was moved past the blade, then forward slightly before the next cut, in the manner of a meat slicer. Microtomes greatly speeded up the preparation of specimens for pathological examination.

Handle

Sturdy tripod stand

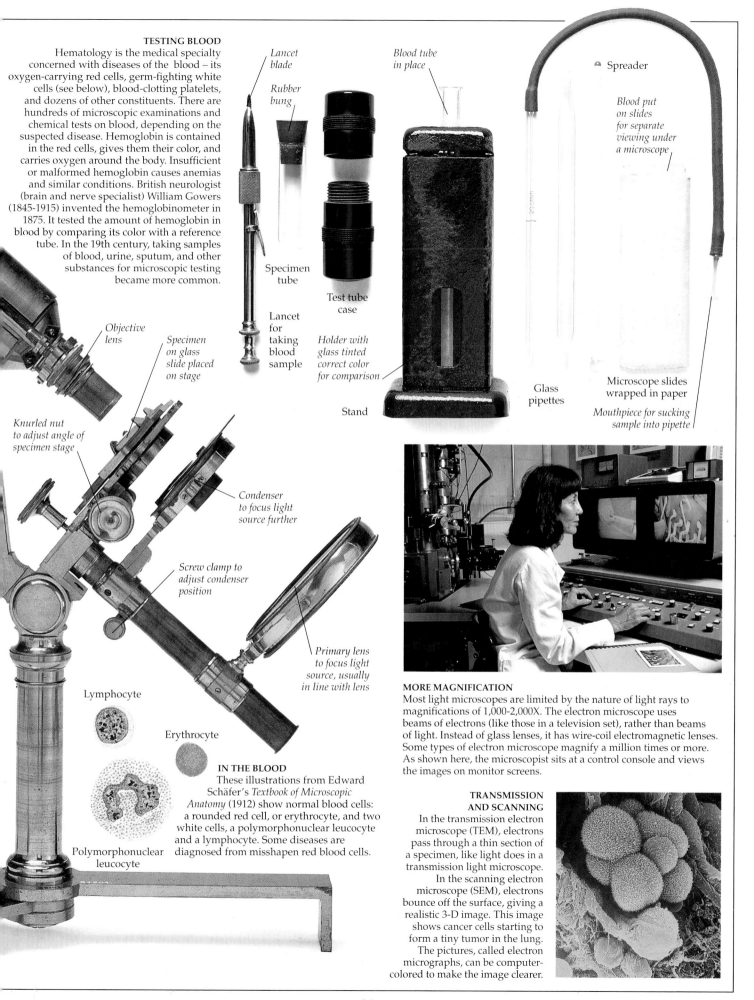

TESTING BLOOD

Hematology is the medical specialty concerned with diseases of the blood – its oxygen-carrying red cells, germ-fighting white cells (see below), blood-clotting platelets, and dozens of other constituents. There are hundreds of microscopic examinations and chemical tests on blood, depending on the suspected disease. Hemoglobin is contained in the red cells, gives them their color, and carries oxygen around the body. Insufficient or malformed hemoglobin causes anemias and similar conditions. British neurologist (brain and nerve specialist) William Gowers (1845-1915) invented the hemoglobinometer in 1875. It tested the amount of hemoglobin in blood by comparing its color with a reference tube. In the 19th century, taking samples of blood, urine, sputum, and other substances for microscopic testing became more common.

Lancet blade

Rubber bung

Blood tube in place

Spreader

Blood put on slides for separate viewing under a microscope

Specimen tube

Lancet for taking blood sample

Test tube case

Holder with glass tinted correct color for comparison

Stand

Glass pipettes

Microscope slides wrapped in paper

Mouthpiece for sucking sample into pipette

Objective lens

Specimen on glass slide placed on stage

Knurled nut to adjust angle of specimen stage

Condenser to focus light source further

Screw clamp to adjust condenser position

Primary lens to focus light source, usually in line with lens

Lymphocyte

Erythrocyte

Polymorphonuclear leucocyte

IN THE BLOOD

These illustrations from Edward Schäfer's *Textbook of Microscopic Anatomy* (1912) show normal blood cells: a rounded red cell, or erythrocyte, and two white cells, a polymorphonuclear leucocyte and a lymphocyte. Some diseases are diagnosed from misshapen red blood cells.

MORE MAGNIFICATION

Most light microscopes are limited by the nature of light rays to magnifications of 1,000-2,000X. The electron microscope uses beams of electrons (like those in a television set), rather than beams of light. Instead of glass lenses, it has wire-coil electromagnetic lenses. Some types of electron microscope magnify a million times or more. As shown here, the microscopist sits at a control console and views the images on monitor screens.

TRANSMISSION AND SCANNING

In the transmission electron microscope (TEM), electrons pass through a thin section of a specimen, like light does in a transmission light microscope. In the scanning electron microscope (SEM), electrons bounce off the surface, giving a realistic 3-D image. This image shows cancer cells starting to form a tiny tumor in the lung. The pictures, called electron micrographs, can be computer-colored to make the image clearer.

Germs and disease

DISEASE CARRIERS
Some germs are spread by personal contact. Others are carried in air or by bad food or water (p. 34). Others are spread by living carriers, or "vectors," especially insects. These suck blood from an infected person, then bite another human and inject some of the germs. The tsetse fly (above) carries the germ *Trypanosoma*, which causes sleeping sickness.

IN THE 19TH CENTURY physicians and scientists came to believe that germs caused many diseases. This replaced the older humoral view (p. 17). The pioneering French microbiologist Louis Pasteur (1822-1895) helped develop the "germ theory" of disease in which bacteria or other microbes are the cause of infectious diseases. In 1876 a German physician, Robert Koch (1843-1910), studied anthrax, an animal disease that also affects humans, and was the first to identify that particular microbes cause particular diseases. In 1888 Pasteur's assistant Emil Roux (1853-1933) studied the bacteria that cause diphtheria and their poisonous by-products, toxins. He showed that the toxins, and not the germs, caused diptheria. Earlier the English physician Edward Jenner (1749-1823) had begun to introduce cowpox fluid into people to protect them from smallpox, although he did not understand why it worked. Modern scientists now understand the body's immune system and the process of immunization. This involves giving the body weak or disabled versions of a germ, so that the body becomes immune to them and can fight future challenges by that germ. Linking germs with disease continues today, with the discovery, for example, that some viruses are implicated in causing certain cancers.

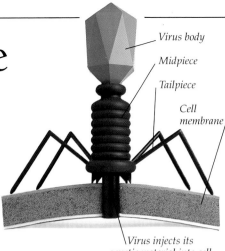

Virus body
Midpiece
Tailpiece
Cell membrane

Virus injects its genetic material into cell

TYPES OF GERMS
"Germ" is the common name for microbes that get into the body, multiply, and cause disease. Viruses are probably the smallest: 254,000 in a line are only 1 in long. Some are round, while others look like space probes (above). Bacteria, which often do not cause disease, are about 100 times bigger, and shaped like balls, rods, or commas. Protists, a type of single-celled organism, are about 0.002 in across.

COWPOX AND SMALLPOX
This horn belonged to a cow used by Jenner to provide cowpox-infected fluid to vaccinate people against smallpox, a more dangerous disease. Variolation – inoculating uninfected people with fluid from pustules of smallpox sufferers – had been common in the East, and spread to Europe by the early 18th century. But it could result in fatal smallpox, so Jenner sought to reduce the risks by using cowpox. His scientific investigations, published in 1798, showed that fluid from a human with cowpox could be used more safely for vaccinations.

Tortoiseshell handle

Ivory blade

LANCET
This vaccination lancet was used by Jenner to introduce fluid from a cowpox sore through a person's skin into the tissues. "Vaccination" comes from *vacca*, Latin for cow.

THE TERROR OF RABIES
Louis Pasteur made many advances in microbiology (the study of microbes, p. 35). He showed that the yeast microbe ferments sugar into alcohol, and contaminating bacteria spoil milk and wine. He devised the pasteurization process to kill them. Hearing of Koch's experiments with anthrax bacteria, Pasteur wondered if it would be possible to produce an anthrax vaccine, as Jenner had done for smallpox. In 1881 he made weakened versions of anthrax bacteria, injected them into animals, then gave the animals full-strength bacteria. The animals survived. In the 1880s he carried out many animal experiments to produce a vaccine against the terrible viral disease rabies. In 1885 he produced a rabies vaccine, made from the spinal cords of rabbits. The first recipient was nine-year-old Joseph Meister, bitten 14 times by a possibly rabid dog. Joseph lived.

VON BEHRING'S VACCINE
German professor Emil von Behring (1854-1917) devised vaccines against diphtheria and tetanus in 1890. They contained not weakened versions of the bacteria, but natural substances called antibodies, which acted against the poison, or toxin, produced by the bacteria. These antibodies were taken from the blood of animals that had been given small doses of diptheria or tetanus toxin. Von Behring used the term "antitoxin" for this type of vaccine. He won the first Nobel Prize for physiology and medicine in 1901.

Growing microbes in the lab

To study bacteria and other germs, Robert Koch would have used equipment similar to the modern items shown on the right. Koch developed the ideas of his teacher, anatomist Jakob Henle (p. 30), and devised the four Henle-Koch postulates, or conditions, which must be fulfilled before an organism (germ) can be said to cause a disease. These are: 1. A specific germ must be taken from sufferers and identified in all cases of the disease. 2. It must be cultured, or grown in pure form, in the laboratory. 3. When given to animals, these cultured germs must cause the disease. 4. The germs must then be recovered from the animals used, showing the germs have survived and multiplied in their host. Modern versions of these guidelines are still in use today.

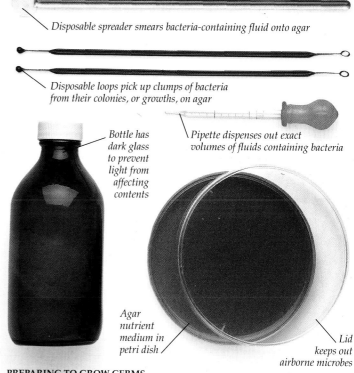

Disposable spreader smears bacteria-containing fluid onto agar

Disposable loops pick up clumps of bacteria from their colonies, or growths, on agar

Pipette dispenses out exact volumes of fluids containing bacteria

Bottle has dark glass to prevent light from affecting contents

Agar nutrient medium in petri dish

Lid keeps out airborne microbes

THE FINAL LINK

This cartoon of 1910 makes a pun about Koch culturing, ("teaching") bacteria. Koch was the first to show that specific germs caused specific diseases. He proved that large rod-shaped bacteria (discovered in 1849) were the cause of the animal and human infection, anthrax. He went on to identify the tuberculosis bacteria in 1882 and the comma bacillus of cholera by 1884. Berlin's Institute for Infectious Diseases was built in his honor, and he received a Nobel Prize in 1905.

PREPARING TO GROW GERMS

Microbes are grown in a nutrient medium. This is a jellylike substance based on agar (seaweed extract) with certain nutrients added. The nutrients feed the microbes. Many disease-causing bacteria thrive in blood, so they are grown on blood agar – blood nutrients in the agar give it a red color. The hot liquid agar is poured into a shallow, circular petri dish, where it sets. The bacteria are plated out – smeared on to the agar – and the dishes are placed in an incubator at body temperature to grow and multiply.

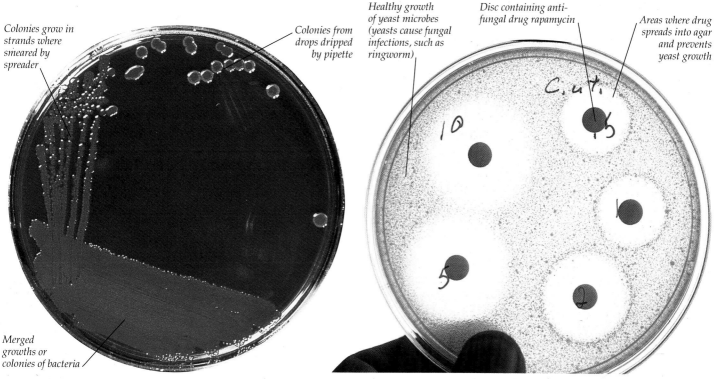

Colonies grow in strands where smeared by spreader

Colonies from drops dripped by pipette

Merged growths or colonies of bacteria

Healthy growth of yeast microbes (yeasts cause fungal infections, such as ringworm)

Disc containing anti-fungal drug rapamycin

Areas where drug spreads into agar and prevents yeast growth

GROWING MICROBES

The individual bacteria (or other germs) feed on the nutrients in the agar. They grow and multiply into millions, forming colonies, or growths, which are visible to the naked eye. As they produce wastes and die, the colony may fade in the center but keeps spreading outward in a ring. Samples from the colonies are picked up by loops and transferred to new dishes of agar.

SELECTING DRUGS TO KILL GERMS

Culture samples are identified by being stained and then examined under a microscope. They can also be put on dishes with different mixtures of nutrients, to see if they grow, or be grown near small pools (wells) or disks containing drugs, as here, to see which drugs inhibit their growth. This is how an effective drug may be chosen for the person who gave the sample.

Public health

By the late 19th century, the Industrial Revolution in Britain had created filthy, overcrowded towns and cities for industrial workers. Encouraged by crowding and poor nutrition, germs spread in contaminated water, food, and air, bringing epidemics of cholera, typhoid, smallpox, tuberculosis, and pneumonia. The importance of clean water was demonstrated in 1854 when Dr. John Snow (1813-1858) discovered that a London outbreak of cholera centered on a water pump. The discovery of germs (pp. 32-33) and disinfection led to more emphasis on cleanliness. The links between poverty and ill health slowly became clear. Britain's Public Health Act, 1848, began the move toward national programs to promote health measures, such as clean water and proper sanitation. By the 1920s the links being made between vitamins in food, and diseases such as rickets, were also showing the need for a balanced diet.

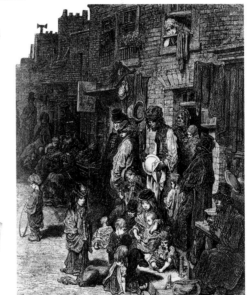

THE SPECTER OF CHOLERA
In this 19th-century illustration, "Cholera tramples the victor and the vanquish'd both." From about 1817 cholera spread west from the Indian subcontinent, and swept repeatedly through the crowded cities of industrial Europe. During the first wave to hit London in 1832, more than 7,000 people died. In America, if cholera was suspected on boats bringing in European immigrants, mobs turned them away at dockside.

FILTHY CONDITIONS
The condition of the urban poor, as shown in this picture of the Whitechapel district in London, by Gustave Doré (1832-1883), became a subject for social and reforming concern during the 19th century. From 1837 national statistics on births and the causes and places of death were gathered, which allowed links to be made between living and working conditions and particular diseases.

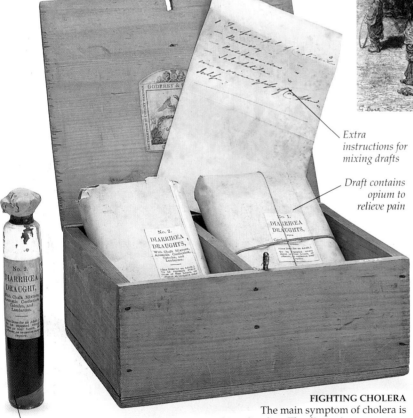

Extra instructions for mixing drafts

Draft contains opium to relieve pain

No. 2.
DIARRHŒA DRAUGHTS,
With Chalk Mixture, Aromatic Confection, Catechu, and Laudanum.

No. 1.
DIARRHŒA DRAUGHTS,

No. 2.
DIARRHŒA DRAUGHT,

Draft contains catechu to shrink the swollen lining of the intestines

FIGHTING CHOLERA
The main symptom of cholera is copious, watery, gushing diarrhea. The disease's name comes from *kholera*, the Greek term for diarrhea. The intestinal contents are expelled, followed by bits of inflamed intestinal lining. If sufferers try to drink or eat, they become violently sick. The loss of fluids and body salts soon causes weakness and prostration. This cholera medicine chest from the second half of the 19th century contains two types of "diarrhea drafts," which aimed to calm the digestive system and ease the abdominal pain.

Removeable lid for filling

CLEAN WATER
One practical result of the discovery of germs, and how they could spread in water supplies, was the water filter. This model from the late 19th-early 20th century consists of a large glazed earthenware jar containing a filter element made of carbon. Microbes and other tiny items stuck to the carbon particles, which were replaced regularly. Modern water purifiers work in the same way using layers of activated carbon. Today, in developed countries, water is usually purified at the sources of supply, rather than when it reaches individual homes. However, millions of people in poorer countries still do not have access to clean water, and cholera epidemics sometimes follow natural disasters, such as floods and earthquakes.

Zinc tap

High-level
water cistern

Working
model of
Jenning's
water closet
c. 1900

*Broth remains
uncontaminated*

DOWN THE PAN

Water washed away waste
in the public lavatories
of ancient Rome (p. 18).
The principle of the flush
lavatory was devised by
John Harrington in about
1590, mainly to get rid of the
smells. But very few houses
had water pipes to refill the
cistern or a proper drain to
empty the pan. It was easier
to dig a pit at the end of the
garden, or in a city to dump
the slops into a nearby
waterway. The modern
lavatory was developed
in stages from about
1770, culminating in the
low-level syphonic version
in 1915. The widespread
introduction of lavatories
could impose a strain on
what were often quite
limited sewage disposal
systems. But by the 1880s,
many of the major cities
had new treatment plants
using chemicals and
mechanical agitation to
purify waste. The one in
Nottingham, England, was
so impressive that foreign
visitors went to see it.

Outlet to drain

*Sealed end
prevents air
from entering*

Flask filled
with boiled
broth

ARMY HEALTH

In the Boer War (1899-1902), five times more
soldiers died from disease than from battle injuries.
Improved health measures were soon adopted by
the army, with the aim of producing healthier
troops for a better chance of victory, and cutting the
numbers dying from typhoid and other preventable
diseases. Mass immunization, clean water, and
good food, meant that far fewer died from disease
in the Russian-Japanese War of 1904-1905.

GERMS IN THE AIR

In the late 19th century, the new germ theory
(p. 32) was used to explain the epidemics of
disease in industrial towns. Previously, "miasmas"
– inanimate noxious exhalations from rotting matter
or stagnant water – had been seen as responsible. Louis
Pasteur (1822-1895) argued that germs were the cause of
decay, and also of many diseases. He undertook several
experiments to show that germs are present in the air and
will grow in a sterile nutrient medium (p. 33) if they gain
access to it. To prove his theories, he boiled broth in glass
flasks and sealed the ends to prevent air from entering. The
broth stayed unspoiled until they were opened, which proved
Pasteur's theories. Pasteur then did experiments to find out if germs
spread more easily in certain environments.
He showed that there were fewer germs
in the cleaner, thinner air at the tops
of mountains than in the air in
crowded, dirty towns, where
disease spread rapidly.

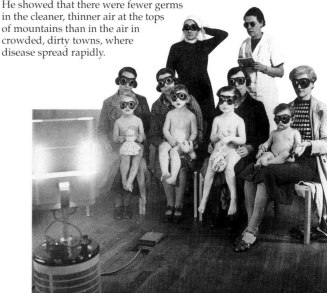

LIGHT RELIEF

Ultraviolet light therapy was made available in many industrial
areas during the 1930s. Here, it is given in a British child welfare
clinic, 1938, to prevent rickets, a condition caused by a lack of
vitamin D, in which bones do not form properly. Rickets is caused
by a poor diet and a lack of sunlight. Sunlight causes vitamin D to
form in the skin, so ultraviolet light (which is also in sunlight) can
be used to do the same thing.

Fads and fashions

MANY PEOPLE THINK THAT SCIENCE progresses steadily, in a logical fashion. New theories are tested by experiments, then accepted or discarded. Improved methods and techniques replace older ones. But in reality, scientific knowledge develops in fits and starts, with many false trails and dead ends. In addition to the truly eccentric, various ideas with the flimsiest scientific basis have become medically fashionable for a time, then faded away. This book shows dozens of medical practices, such as leeching (p. 26), that are no longer in use. Yet respected physicians believed in them, and patients were ready to undergo treatment. Advances in other branches of science have also affected medicine. The invention of the electrical cell, or battery, in 1800 by Alessandro Volta, for example, led to a variety of treatments using electricity, most of which have been abandoned. Are we any different today? We may think so. Medical scientists usually require good evidence that a new technique really does work before it becomes widespread. But in a century's time, people may look back at some of our medical tests and treatments and smile wryly.

THE QUACK DOCTOR
The word "quack" came from the 16th-century term quacksalver, meaning someone who sold salves, balms, and other healing preparations by fast-talking patter or "quacking." Many quacksalvers were not doctors at all, but traveling salesmen. Luckily for them, but not for the patients, they were no longer around when the magic cure-all potion was found to be worthless.

ELECTRICITY FOR TB
The lung disease tuberculosis (TB) was known to Hippocrates (pp. 16-17) as *phthisis*. It was widespread in the 19th and early 20th centuries. The only treatment was rest, good food, and lots of sun and fresh air. The discovery of electricity gave rise to many experimental electrical treatments for various diseases, including TB, as shown here.

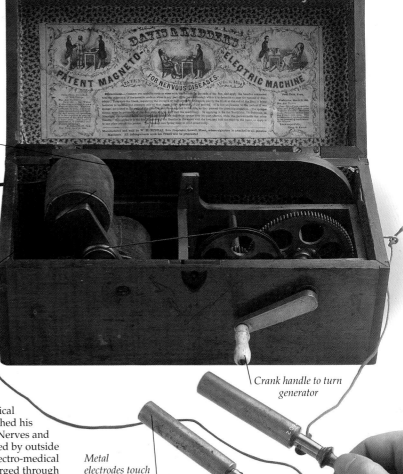

Horseshoe magnet

Held in hand

Brass tractor

Points put on skin

Silver tractor

GALVANIC TRACTORS
As Luigi Galvani experimented with electricity (see below), he found that a combination of brass and silver rods seemed to produce the strongest muscle twitch. These "galvanic tractors" aimed to mimic his animal experiments on the human body, and to redirect the electricity to cure conditions such as numbness, muscle weakness, and gout.

Spinning wire coils of electrical generator

Crank handle to turn generator

CHARGING THE BODY
In the late 18th century, Luigi Galvani (1737-1798) discovered "animal electricity." In fact, he unknowingly made a simple electrical cell (battery) when his metal knives and other equipment touched his freshly dissected animals, causing their muscles to twitch. (Nerves and muscles work by tiny electrical currents, and they can be stimulated by outside electricity.) Soon electrical treatments were the fashion. This electro-medical machine from the 1850s generated low voltage, which was discharged through the body as an electrical shock from the two metal electrodes.

Metal electrodes touch the patient's skin

Wide-bore brass
needle inserted
through anus

Screw fitting to
remove needle
for refilling

Brass syringe barrel

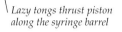

Levers pushed
together

CLEANING OUT

Since the time of ancient Egypt, the enema – introducing liquid into the rectum (lower bowel) – has had a proud history. Enemas are used today before certain types of surgery, to wash out the lower bowel as a hygienic measure, and to introduce medications or body salts and minerals into the body. In the past they were advised for all manner of ailments, even slight indigestion or headache.

Enema syringe
(probably 18th century)

Lazy tongs thrust piston
along the syringe barrel

Handle

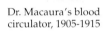

Vibrating rubber
tip applied to body

BETTER CIRCULATION

All body parts need a good supply of circulating blood to bring oxygen and nutrients and to take away waste products. The mechanical massager was cranked like a hand drill, and its vibrating tip placed on the body surface to massage the region below. Modern massage and therapy methods recognize the importance of good circulation, and of relaxing tense muscles and exercising stiff joints. Certain forms of gentle vibro-massage and heat massage are used today to improve the circulation of the blood.

Rotating
weights

Fixed (non-spinning) shaft

Dr. Macaura's blood
circulator, 1905-1915

Handle and crank

SMOKING IS GOOD FOR YOU?

Millions of people still smoke tobacco, despite its well-publicized links with heart and circulatory disorders, breathing and lung problems, and cancers. Tobacco reached Europe from North America in the 16th century, and was smoked for its stimulant qualities (caused by the addictive drug nicotine). This tobacco resuscitator kit from 1774 was used to revive "persons apparently dead" by either using the bellows to blow tobacco smoke up the rectum, or into the lungs through the nose or mouth. Tobacco enemas were popular from the 17th to early 19th centuries.

TAKING THE WATERS

The Greeks and Romans considered bathing to be healthy. Then in the medieval period, cleanliness was distrusted. In the 18th century, baths returned to fashion. Many spas and springs became famed for mineral-rich waters, odors, and reputed healing powers. America's first health resort was set up in 1774 in Saratoga Springs, NY. It took its name from the Mohawk Indian for "place of the medicine waters of the great spring."

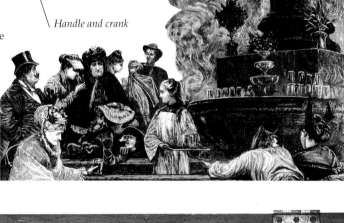

Flask

Curved silver
pipe for
inflating
the lungs

Tobacco box

Rectal tubes
attach to
tobacco chamber

Chamber for
burning tobacco
attaches to bellows

Flexible
connecting
tube

Lever for
filling bellows
with air

Bellows

Nostril pipes
attach to
tobacco
chamber

Syringe for
injecting
cordials into
the stomach

Seeing into the body

I<small>N</small> 1895 <small>THE</small> G<small>ERMAN</small> <small>PHYSICIST</small> Wilhelm Röntgen (1845-1923) discovered X-rays (X for "unknown"). They could pass through soft materials, including human flesh, but were blocked by hard, dense substances, such as bone. Suddenly doctors could look inside the body without cutting it open. Within a few months, X-ray photographs (radiographs) were revealing broken bones, swallowed coins, embedded bullets, and gallstones. The harmful effects of X-rays on living tissues were soon noticed, and by the 1900s they were being used to treat cancerous tumors (radiotherapy, p. 53). By the 1950s, the safe use of X-rays for diagnosis had been well defined. Since the 1970s, a new generation of medical imagers has produced ever more detailed pictures of the body's interior. They all scan the body – moving a beam back and forth to create two-dimensional image "slices." They do this many times and rely on a computer to assemble 3-D pictures of body parts.

BEING SCANNED
From the outside, modern scanners look like most other large-scale machinery. The CT scanner resembles a huge washing machine. The patient lies on a movable bed as the scanning beams rotate inside the machinery casing. The operator watches the resulting images "live" on TV screens. The X-rays used by this scanner are in very low doses, minimizing the radiation risk for patients.

INVISIBLE X-RAYS
The X-ray tube was a development of the cathode ray or vacuum tube, used in the late 19th century to probe the structure of the atom. This Jackson X-ray tube (1896) is a very early example. A high voltage was applied to the negative cathode and positive anode. Subatomic particles called electrons streamed from the cathode. (Cathode rays are really beams of electrons, p. 31). When they hit the anode, their energy changed into invisible X-rays, which passed out through the glass.

Air pumped out from here during manufacture

Electrons strike the anode and X-rays are given off

Electrons are accelerated from the cathode

X-Ray tube, 1896

No air or other gases inside tube

Portable ECG machine, 1946

Lead to plug

Electrodes

Transfers pulse to wand

Stylus scratches trace onto smoked paper in carriage wand

Carriage wand holds paper

Modified Marey sphygmograph, c. 1870

Plate rests on radial (wrist) artery

Screw adjusts pressure on artery

Clockwork motor moves carriage along

MEASURING BLOOD PRESSURE
The sphygmograph traces a wavy line that represents a record of blood pressure and pulse over time. The first practical, portable version was devised in 1860 by the French physician Etienne-Jules Marey (1830-1904) and was strapped to the wrist. Modern battery-powered types are still used for physiological research and to help detect heart and circulatory problems, but they have largely been replaced by sphygmomanometers (p. 61).

THE ECG TRACE
On an ECG trace, called an electrocardiogram, a pen marks the line on a moving strip of paper. Each heartbeat shows as a pattern of spikes and dips called the P, Q, R, S, and T waves. In a normal resting adult, the whole beat takes less than a second. The trace can also be displayed on a screen and recorded by photography or video.

Seconds

0   0.2   0.4   0.6

R

P   Q   S   T

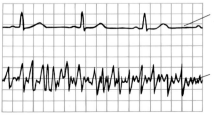

Standard pattern of waves shows electrical pulses are coordinated and heart is beating at regular intervals

Irregular pattern shows electrical pulses are uncoordinated and heart is twitching rather than beating

ECG AND EEG
The electrocardiograph (ECG) detects and records the tiny electrical signals which coordinate the heart's beats, and which can indicate heart disorders. The signals "ripple" outward and are picked up by metal sensors stuck to the skin. Willem Einthoven (1860-1927) developed the ECG during the 1900s. The first filled two rooms and needed five technicians. Portable ECGs date from 1928. Recordings of the brain's electrical activity are made in a similar way, by the electroencephalograph (EEG), which came into use in the 1930s.

APT SCANNING
In applied potential tomography (APT), now renamed electrical impedance tomography, electrodes attached to the body send out, or apply, tiny electrical signals. Other electrodes pick these up, and the changes in their strength and timing are analyzed by computer to create a picture. This original piece of research equipment from 1987 was used in Britain. It was suggested years ago, like most scanning technologies, but had to wait for the high-speed, inexpensive calculating power of the modern computer.

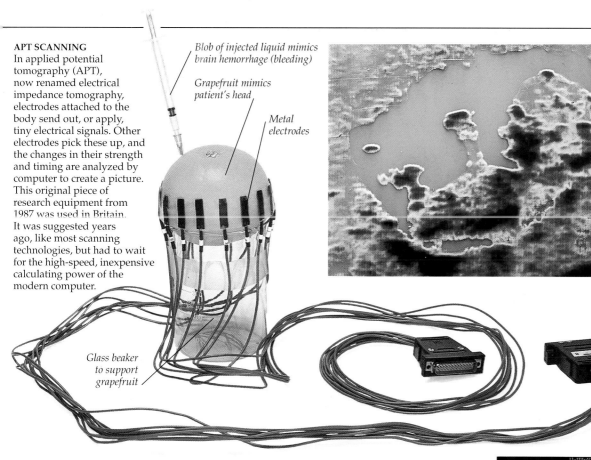

Blob of injected liquid mimics brain hemorrhage (bleeding)

Grapefruit mimics patient's head

Metal electrodes

Glass beaker to support grapefruit

Plug connects electrodes to computer via multiplexing interface unit

ULTRASOUND
High-pitched sound waves (too shrill for our ears) are beamed from a combined emitter-receiver into the body, then reflected by various tissues. The receiver detects the echoes and feeds the results into the computer and display. Developed in the 1950s, ultrasound is now routine for imaging the beating heart, and babies in the womb, as here. Over 25 percent of all of today's hospital imaging is by ultrasound.

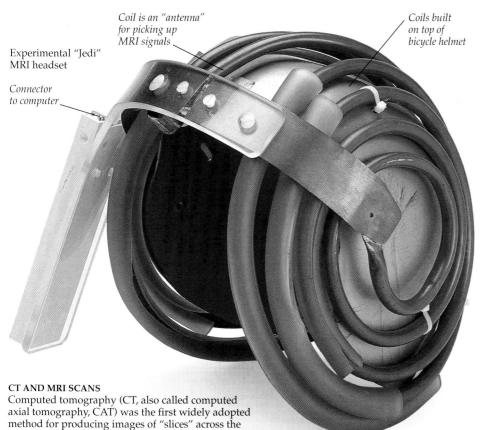

Experimental "Jedi" MRI headset

Connector to computer

Coil is an "antenna" for picking up MRI signals

Coils built on top of bicycle helmet

MR IMAGE
Computer color-coding helps doctors to interpret the scanner's images. In this MRI "slice" through the head, parts of the brain are colored green, yellow, and red. These correspond to the water content of the different brain tissues.

HOW MRI WORKS
MRI works on the hydrogen atoms in the body's water molecules (H_2O). These atoms usually spin in different directions. The MR machine emits a strong magnetic field, making the spinning hydrogen atoms line up.

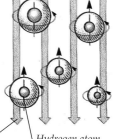

Magnetic field

Hydrogen atom

Pulse of radio waves

DETECTING RADIO WAVES
A pulse of radio waves is then sent through the body. This makes the atoms tilt slightly. Before the atoms realign they produce weak radio signals, which are detected and analyzed to produce an image.

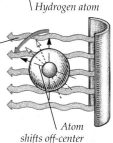

Atom shifts off-center

CT AND MRI SCANS
Computed tomography (CT, also called computed axial tomography, CAT) was the first widely adopted method for producing images of "slices" across the body. An X-ray source and detector move around the body and the resulting signals (proportional to the density of body organs) are processed into pictures by the scanner's computer. Magnetic imaging (MRI, originally called nuclear resonance imaging, NMR) builds up pictures in a similar way but derives from the magnetic behavior of water molecules inside the body. MRI is used to diagnose diseases and injuries affecting the brain, nerves, bones, muscles, and internal organs, especially the liver. This "Jedi" helmet was an experimental device designed to get the best possible pictures of a child's brain.

The natural pharmacy

A MEDICINAL DRUG IS ANY SUBSTANCE TAKEN to prevent or diagnose a disease, to relieve symptoms, or treat an underlying disease process. From ancient beginnings (pp. 12-13), drug therapy gradually became based on science as well as craft. Pharmacists and scientists began to select certain parts of a plant, crush or dissolve them, and treat them with chemicals to extract a purer form of the drug – the "active ingredient." The aims were to make its actions more powerful and specific, with fewer side effects, and to make it easier and safer to take in the form of a professionally prepared potion or pill. For centuries the main reference works on natural drugs were the ancient herbals (p. 21). Later came the early pharmacopoeias, which were official lists of approved drugs that were prepared for a country, city, or organization.

STORING DRUGS

The 16th-century pharmacist boiled, crushed, ground, and dissolved herbs and other plant products to make preparations that were often stored in jars as dried powders or in oils. *Olio mirtine* (myrtle oil) was made by dissolving myrtle berries in the oil from unripe olives. In 1691 one W. Salmon stated that it "strengthens weak Limbs and Joynts, fastens loose Gums . . . fastens the Hair . . . strengthens the Brain, Nerves, and Stomach, stays Vomiting, and stops Fluxes."

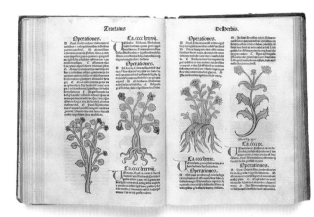

THE HERBALS

Herbals, such as this German example of 1491, *Hortus Sanitatis* ("Garden of Health"), were used by doctors and public alike. They often included preparations made from birds, fish, and other animals. One of the most popular was *The English Physitian* (1652) by Nicholas Culpeper. The pharmacopoeias, the first of which was published in Florence in 1498, were official civic guides for doctors and gave lists of approved drugs, with information on their uses, doses, and side effects. In the 16th century many European cities prepared their own. In some places, doctors were legally bound to use them. First published in 1820, the *United States Pharmacopoeia* became the legal standard by enactment of the Food and Drug Act in 1906.

WEIGHING, PULVERIZING, RECORDING, DISCUSSING

In this scene from a 16th-century pharmacy, a customer discusses requirements with the chief apothecary (chemist-pharmacist), who is weighing out a substance with handheld scales. Various dried herbs and animal parts are stored in hanging muslin bags, while products preserved in oil are kept in glazed jars. A lowly assistant pulverizes material in a mortar and pestle, while a senior assistant records new recipes. The row of jars on the lowest shelf is for aqueous (water-based) extracts of herbs and other chemicals.

White willow leaves
Salix alba

DRUGS COPIED FROM NATURE

From the early 19th century, apothecaries began to investigate drugs systematically, and to isolate by chemical means their active principles. In 1829 white willow, traditionally used to treat fever, pain, and inflammation, was one of the first plants to have its active ingredient extracted. By 1852 the ingredient had been made artificially in a laboratory, and by 1899 its derivative was being sold to the public as aspirin.

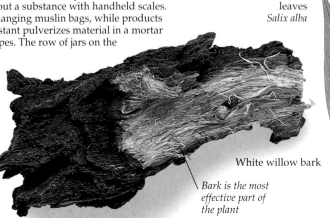

White willow bark

Bark is the most effective part of the plant

HELPING THE PATIENT

Like physicians and surgeons (p. 25), the apothecary separated from other trades, such as alchemists and greengrocers, and came under the control of professional institutions, such as London's Society of Apothecaries, founded in 1617. Apothecaries and pharmacists have often filled the gap between fully qualified physicians affordable only by the rich, and the folk healers and untrained quacks.

MAKING PILLS

Pills are small balls of medicinal substances. Tablets are newer inventions made by mechanical means; they are flatter, usually dry, and more compressed. Before automatic pill-making machines, pills were laboriously prepared by hand. The herb or other source was used whole, usually in powdered form, or treated to extract the active ingredients. These were all weighed out extremely carefully, so that each pill contained the same dose. Some pharmacists became famed for the quality and horrible taste of their pills. The bitterest medicine was thought to do the most good.

Handle   *Balance beam*

1 WEIGHING THE INGREDIENTS
This set of balancing scales from the early 19th century was used to weigh raw materials. The pharmacist held up the scales by the handle, with the pans suspended on strings. Small weights were placed on one pan, and balanced by spooning the powdered preparation on to the other one.

Weights   *Brass pan*

Sliding rail   *Tray for roughly-shaped pills*   *Ridged lower section of mold corresponds to ridged upper section*

1   4   6   12   18   24

Ridged upper section of mold (face up)

Flat, circular shapes fall into tray, cut from "sausages" by grooves in base and wooden cutter

"Sausages" placed on top of brass cutting plate

2 FASHIONING THE PILLS
The weighed-out ingredients were mixed with inactive substances, such as mineral clays, yeast extracts, and powdered roots like marshmallow. These gave volume and provided shape and texture. From these ingredients, a doughlike paste was made, rolled into an even sausage shape on the flat pill-making board, and placed on the ridged lower section (in the opposite direction to the ridges). The upper, ridged part was pushed over the top, cutting the "sausage" into flat shapes.

Ingredients rolled out into even pieces on flat board

Flat wooden cutter, also with grooved cutting plate, is run over sausage shapes

How the pill-making machine worked

Marble slab for rolling paste

3 FINISHING THE PILLS
The flat shapes were molded into spherical pills by rolling them gently under the fingers on the tray of the pill-rounder, or pill-finisher.

Raised lip to prevent pills from rolling off

19th-century boxwood pill-rounder

4 COATING THE PILLS
Since pills were usually moist, they tended to stick together, so they were sprinkled with a coating, or rolled in the coating inside the pill-coater (pill-silverer). Dry coatings included sugar, ground-up roots such as licorice, talc, and even the colorful spores of stagshorn moss. Silver and gold were used to cover pills for wealthy customers, to make them look more important and attractive.

19th-century boxwood pill-coater

Pills

Tight-fitting lid forms complete spherical chamber for swirling and rolling pills in coating

Modern drugs

Dᴜʀɪɴɢ ᴛʜᴇ 19ᴛʜ ᴄᴇɴᴛᴜʀʏ, ᴘʜᴀʀᴍᴀᴄᴏʟᴏɢʏ, the study of how drugs affect the body, became a full scientific specialty (pp. 40-41). At the beginning of the 20th century, new chemical techniques were applied to drugs, and the first synthetic (non-natural) drugs were produced. This is chemotherapy, which was pioneered by the German researcher Paul Ehrlich (1854-1915). In 1910 he synthesized the chemical salvarsan, which was used to treat the venereal disease syphilis. It was the first drug to be made in the laboratory specifically to treat the cause of a disease. In 1928 Alexander Fleming (1881-1955), a Scottish researcher, discovered the bacteria-killing properties of a substance made by the mold (fungus) called *Penicillium*. From this came penicillin and other antibiotic drugs, which fight infections and save millions of lives. By the 1950s a huge pharmaceutical industry had arisen, designing, making, and testing drugs. Since the 1970s, there has been a revival of "green medicine" and studying plants for potential drugs. About one-third of modern packaged medicines are still based on plants.

MAGIC BULLETS
In 1908 Ehrlich was awarded a Nobel Prize for work on how body defences fight disease and infection. This is called immunology. He aimed to find drugs that were as effective against microbes as the body's own antibodies. He called them "magic bullets" as he imagined them shooting straight at the microbes and killing them, leaving the rest of the body entirely unharmed.

FLEMING, FLOREY, AND PENICILLIN
Working at St. Mary's Hospital, London, Alexander Fleming noticed that mold had grown on a culture medium (p. 33) in the laboratory and killed the bacteria breeding in it. He named the substance penicillin. The Australian pathologist Howard Florey (1898-1968) took up the work and helped develop large-scale production of penicillin, in time for use in the Second World War (1914-1918).

Active ingredient taken from stem and flower

Howard Florey

Madagascar periwinkle
Catharanthus roseus

ANTICANCER AGENTS
Like the European greater periwinkle, the Madagascar periwinkle was a traditional remedy for diabetes, which results from a lack of insulin (p. 43). Now researchers have isolated from it two chemicals, vincristine and vinblastine, and used them to treat cancers affecting white blood cells (p. 31) called leukemias. Only a fraction of plants from the world's forests and wild places have so far been examined for medicinal use – another powerful argument for the conservation of nature.

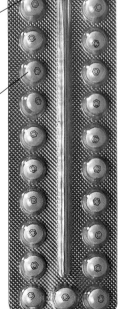

Batch code for manufacturer's checks

Pills made of synthetic (laboratory produced) hormones

Plunger

Syringe containing vaccine

Sheath for needle

Sterile packaging

READY TO INJECT
Several modern technologies come together in this sealed packet. It contains a single disposable syringe, pre-filled with the correct quantity of hepatitis B vaccine, produced from yeast cells that have been altered with genes in the laboratory (p. 63). The sterile container and once-only use avoid spreading infections, such as HIV and hepatitis B, which might otherwise happen by re-using needles or syringes. The vaccine (p. 32) provides protection against the hepatitis B virus, which mainly affects the liver. Vaccination is advised for people working or traveling to areas where the infection is common.

THE PILL
The oral contraceptive pill, known as "The Pill," was developed during the 1950s, based on substances obtained from the Mexican wild yam. These were used to make synthetic hormones, which could alter the female menstrual cycle, usually controlled by the body's natural sex hormones. Several types of oral contraceptive now exist taken on a daily basis.

IN THE LAB
Drug discovery and research is a multibillion-dollar business. However, of perhaps 100,000 chemicals synthesized and tested, only one or two may get through to trials on patients. Researchers work daily with unfamiliar chemicals and potentially harmful microbes, so they must be scrupulous with hygiene and protective measures, and the drugs are checked continually for purity. During initial trials on human volunteers, all effects are carefully monitored. If the tests go well, the drug goes on trials of its effectiveness and safety.

Drug in aerosol can; press down to release

WHERE IT'S NEEDED
Asthma is a breathing disorder that is often treated with drugs called bronchodilators. These widen the tiny airways in the lungs, called bronchioles, which become very narrow in asthma sufferers. Rather than swallow or inject the drug, when it would spread all around the body, the inhaler is a fast and effective way of delivering the drug directly to its target. The user presses the aerosol container, and breathes in deeply at the same time, to "puff and suck" a fine mist of drug deep into the lungs.

Mouthpiece cover

Drug delivery

There are many ways to deliver a drug, or get it into the body. The various routes include being taken by mouth (oral), through the skin via the body surface (topical), injected under the skin (subcutaneous), injected directly into a vein (intravenous), or injected into a muscle (intramuscular). Each route has its advantages, depending on the dose and volume of the drug, whether it enters the tissues quickly or slowly, whether it is needed body-wide, or only in a certain place, and how often it is required. Some substances, such as insulin (see below), are digested in the stomach and made ineffective, so they cannot be taken by the oral route.

Disposable syringe containing insulin

Presser moves slowly along screw thread and pushes syringe piston

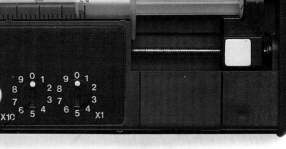

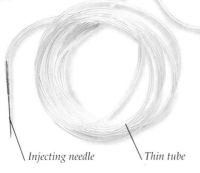

Injecting needle

Pen cover

Injecting needle

Thin tube

Control knobs for dose and speed

INSULIN PEN
The convenient insulin pen, for people with diabetes, injects a small amount of insulin solution each time it is pressed. The dose of insulin can be varied by choosing different amounts and/or concentrations of insulin solution. Since the pen should have only one user, the problem of spreading infections to others should not occur. However, the hollow hypodermic needle, which penetrates below the skin, must be cleaned or changed regularly to avoid contamination with dirt and germs.

Holder for vial of vaccine

Multishot inoculation gun, 1980

Injection head

Trigger

IMPORTANCE OF TIMING
Diabetes results from a lack of the hormone insulin, which controls blood sugar levels. In 1921-1922 in Canada, Frederick Banting (1891-1941) and Charles Best (1899-1978) discovered that animal insulin could replace missing human insulin and restore diabetic patients to health. This 1980s battery-operated pump injects insulin slowly and continuously, mimicking the body's own natural slow production of the hormone.

MULTIPLE INJECTIONS
Multishot inoculation guns were designed to give hundreds of people a small dose of vaccine or drug. The medication is forced through the skin at high pressure without using a needle. First used in a smallpox eradication campaign in 1968, they were soon replaced with much simpler syringes that could be sterilized and reused. Disposable equipment is now used (p. 63).

Dial shows how many doses have been used

SLOW, CONSTANT DELIVERY
Adhesive skin patches stick painlessly to the skin, and the drug seeps slowly through the skin into the blood stream. Only drugs that dissolve through the oily, fatty skin surface can be delivered like this. Another delivery method is the depot injection, where a thick blob of drug in a carrier substance is injected under the skin. This dissolves slowly to release the drug in small, continuous quantities over weeks.

Press to release insulin

Holder for carbon dioxide gas cartridge (power supply)

Alternative treatments

ALTHOUGH TODAY'S ORTHODOX WESTERN MEDICINE uses scientifically tested drugs and surgery, many other systems of medicine still survive from different times and places around the world. People in developed countries may consider them to be a nonconventional or second choice, but many, such as acupuncture or herbalism, have long histories and are considered to be mainstream treatments in their places of origin. Other medical systems, such as homeopathy, are more recent. Alternative techniques may be based on rational theories, or tend to mysticism, yet each claims success and supporters. Some are tried when orthodox medicine has failed. Many appeal because they are holistic, dealing with the whole person – body, mind, and spirit – rather than solely treating symptoms or conditions. As time passes, some alternative therapies, such as osteopathy, become more widely accepted and are adopted into the mainstream, and new ones arise while others gradually fade.

CRYSTALS
Crystals and gems have often been held in awe and claimed to possess medicinal powers. In science, they are used in lasers and to transform vibrations into electricity. Some people believe they may affect the unseen vibrational energies of the human body to heal and cure.

Lavender flowers

Tops distilled to make scented oil

Lavender oil

YOGA – BODY AND MIND
Yoga and similar activities, such as t'ai chi and aikido, have been used to treat medical conditions, but are also ways of improving health of body and mind. Yoga has been practiced in India for over 6,000 years. It focuses on body posture, breathing, and meditation. The postures, called *asanas*, are designed to keep the body supple and promote mind-body harmony. Various types of yoga are used for problems such as stress, depression, arthritis, and digestive upsets.

Fresh chamomile plant *Matricaria chamomilla*

Homeopathic tablets

HOMEOPATHY – LIKE CURES LIKE
The German doctor Samuel Hahnemann (1755-1843) claimed that if large doses of a drug, or chemical, produced symptoms resembling a particular disease, then very small doses of the same drug could treat the disease. He founded homeopathy based on this idea that "like cures like." He researched quinine for malaria first, and then tested many other substances, and claimed that their healing effects increased with dilution. Homeopathic remedies are made from plants, such as chamomile (used for pain relief among other things), minerals, and animal products, diluted hundreds or thousands of times, usually presented in lactose (milk sugar) tablets.

Mother tincture (strong infusion of chamomile in alcohol)

Diluted tincture

Further diluted tincture

AROMATHERAPY
Aromatherapy, intended to appeal to our sense of smell, uses essential oils, or "aromatic essences." These are volatile, oily, fragrant substances obtained from plants in a variety of ways, such as pressing, tapping, distilling, and dissolving. The essential oils are blended with vegetable oils and massaged into the skin while also being breathed in. Sometimes they are given by inhalation alone. Each oil is reputed to have its own therapeutic applications. Aromatherapy is used for breathing problems, pain, urogenital disorders, and mental and emotional problems.

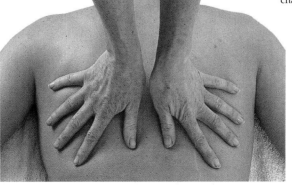

MASSAGING THE BODY
Massage is a more sophisticated version of such simple, instinctive, and effective actions as rubbing the skin after a bump. It is used mainly on the soft tissues – muscles and inner organs. It aims to promote relaxation and release tensions, and exists in some form in almost every culture in the world. In some eastern regions it is as common as taking a bath. Massage can be used for prevention or treatment, for relaxation of body and mind prior to major events, or simply for enjoyment. It is also used in other methods, such as aromatherapy and physiotherapy.

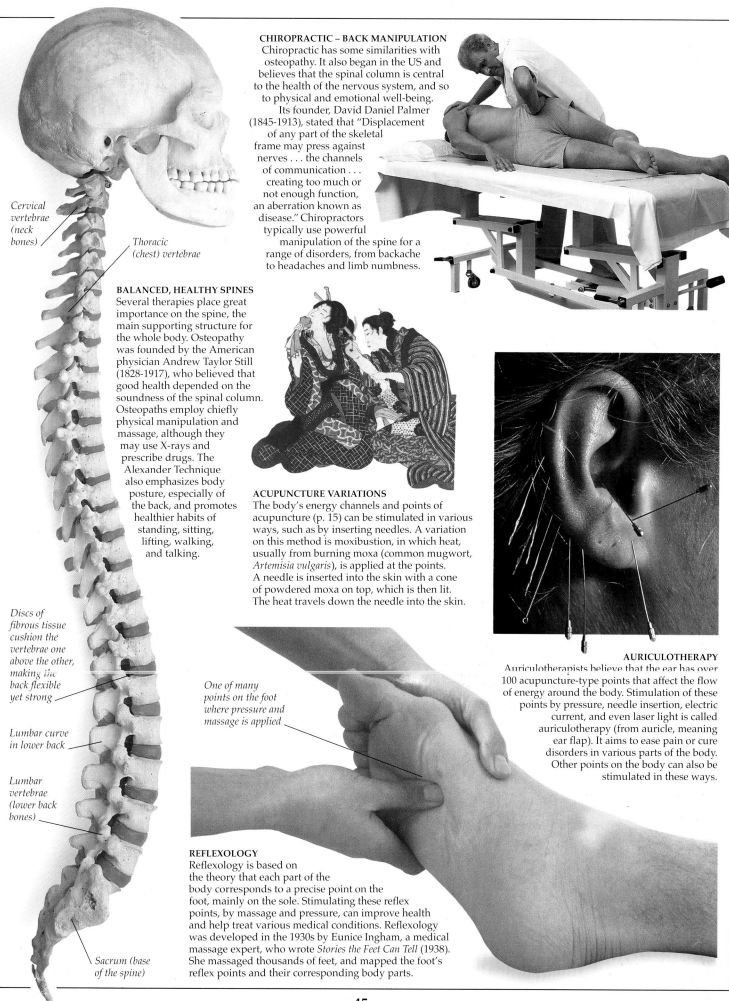

CHIROPRACTIC – BACK MANIPULATION
Chiropractic has some similarities with osteopathy. It also began in the US and believes that the spinal column is central to the health of the nervous system, and so to physical and emotional well-being. Its founder, David Daniel Palmer (1845-1913), stated that "Displacement of any part of the skeletal frame may press against nerves . . . the channels of communication . . . creating too much or not enough function, an aberration known as disease." Chiropractors typically use powerful manipulation of the spine for a range of disorders, from backache to headaches and limb numbness.

Cervical vertebrae (neck bones)

Thoracic (chest) vertebrae

BALANCED, HEALTHY SPINES
Several therapies place great importance on the spine, the main supporting structure for the whole body. Osteopathy was founded by the American physician Andrew Taylor Still (1828-1917), who believed that good health depended on the soundness of the spinal column. Osteopaths employ chiefly physical manipulation and massage, although they may use X-rays and prescribe drugs. The Alexander Technique also emphasizes body posture, especially of the back, and promotes healthier habits of standing, sitting, lifting, walking, and talking.

ACUPUNCTURE VARIATIONS
The body's energy channels and points of acupuncture (p. 15) can be stimulated in various ways, such as by inserting needles. A variation on this method is moxibustion, in which heat, usually from burning moxa (common mugwort, *Artemisia vulgaris*), is applied at the points. A needle is inserted into the skin with a cone of powdered moxa on top, which is then lit. The heat travels down the needle into the skin.

Discs of fibrous tissue cushion the vertebrae one above the other, making the back flexible yet strong

One of many points on the foot where pressure and massage is applied

Lumbar curve in lower back

Lumbar vertebrae (lower back bones)

AURICULOTHERAPY
Auriculotherapists believe that the ear has over 100 acupuncture-type points that affect the flow of energy around the body. Stimulation of these points by pressure, needle insertion, electric current, and even laser light is called auriculotherapy (from auricle, meaning ear flap). It aims to ease pain or cure disorders in various parts of the body. Other points on the body can also be stimulated in these ways.

REFLEXOLOGY
Reflexology is based on the theory that each part of the body corresponds to a precise point on the foot, mainly on the sole. Stimulating these reflex points, by massage and pressure, can improve health and help treat various medical conditions. Reflexology was developed in the 1930s by Eunice Ingham, a medical massage expert, who wrote *Stories the Feet Can Tell* (1938). She massaged thousands of feet, and mapped the foot's reflex points and their corresponding body parts.

Sacrum (base of the spine)

Treating the mind

M ENTAL ILLNESSES AFFECT THE WAY people think, feel, and behave. Such illnesses have probably always existed, as suggested by the ancient operation of trephining the skull (p. 8). However, the scientific diagnosis and treatment of mental illness has a relatively short history, and is still developing. In the Middle Ages the mentally ill lived as outcasts, or under Church care, or chained up in prisonlike hospitals, usually with no hope of recovery. Care and treatment gradually became more humane perhaps partly as a result of the British King George III's periods of insanity from 1765 onward (possibly caused by the disease porphyria). From the 19th century, new types of specialized mental hospitals were set up. Later, medical research showed that many mental problems had a physical basis in abnormal brain structure or chemistry. In the 20th century doctors developed drugs, surgery, and the "talking" treatments, such as pyschoanalysis and cognitive therapy. The specialty concerned with mental illness is now called psychiatry.

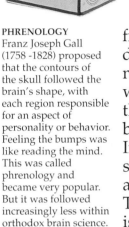

PHRENOLOGY
Franz Joseph Gall (1758 -1828) proposed that the contours of the skull followed the brain's shape, with each region responsible for an aspect of personality or behavior. Feeling the bumps was like reading the mind. This was called phrenology and became very popular. But it was followed increasingly less within orthodox brain science.

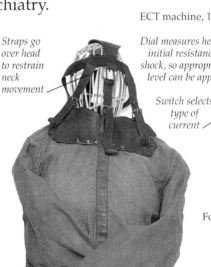

Straps go over head to restrain neck movement

ECT machine, 1950

Dial measures head's initial resistance to shock, so appropriate level can be applied

Switch selects type of current

SHOCK TREATMENT
Following the discovery of the brain's delicate electrical activity, detectable by EEG (p. 38), electroconvulsive therapy (ECT) was first used in 1938. Electric currents were passed through the brain, often causing seizures (convulsions) to shock patients out of severe mental disorder. This therapy was controversial from the start, but is sometimes still used, mainly for severe depression.

BEDLAM IN THE MADHOUSE
London's Bethlem (Bethlehem) Royal Hospital was one of the earliest mental asylums, admitting its first "lunatics" in 1377. Its name gave us the word *bedlam*, meaning noisy and chaotic. In the 18th century particularly, it was a popular pastime for the healthy to visit the madhouse and be entertained by the suffering of the inmates. One of the first books to describe mental illness in detail was *On the Signs of Possession* by the German physician Johann Wyer (1515-1588).

Needle goes through skin and muscles of back, into fluid around spinal cord

RESTRAINING PATIENTS
Straitjackets were designed to prevent patients from injuring themselves or others. The French doctor Philippe Pinel (1745-1826) suggested that restraint made dangerous behavior more likely. He proposed a "moral treatment" – gaining the patient's confidence by appealing to his or her underlying rationality by gentle means or, if necessary, by being authoritative. Then he tried to rid the patient of the mistaken idea in their brain that was causing the illness, through work, music, or an experience to discredit the idea.

Straitjacket, 1930

Syringe can be connected here to take fluid sample

Cerebrospinal manometer

TOO MUCH PRESSURE
The cerebrospinal fluid surrounds and nourishes both the brain and the spinal cord. Disturbances in its volume, pressure, or constituents can affect the brain, and show up in behavioral changes. This equipment measures the pressure of cerebrospinal fluid.

Height of fluid in bore indicates pressure of cerebrospinal fluid

PROBING THE UNCONSCIOUS
Psychoanalysis was founded as a branch of medicine by the Viennese doctor Sigmund Freud (1856-1939). The analyst interviews the patient, encouraging them to talk openly about their innermost thoughts and emotions. This is called "free association" and is designed to help patients identify subconscious worries and conflicts that may be causing the problems. Raising such thoughts to a conscious level helps the patient to deal with them and may help to clear the problem. Freud based his theories on the importance of sexuality. Other people developed other theories. Alfred Adler (1870-1937) based his ideas on the importance of individual power, or lack of it; Carl Jung (1875-1961) divided people into personality types, and did not emphasize sexuality.

FROM MIND TO CANVAS
Creative activities such as painting, sculpture, and music can help people with mental illness in two ways. One way is to express their behavioral difficulties and emotional conflicts in a different, more physical form. Experts then assess the products and attempt to diagnose the problem and its underlying causes. The other way is to "externalize" the mental problem; that is, to transfer it from the mind to an external object or process. As part of therapy, this may help to reduce or remove the problem.

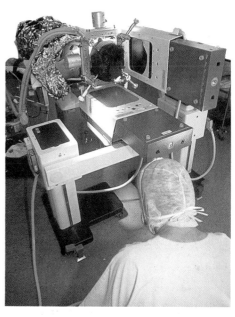

RESEARCHING THE BRAIN
Our knowledge of brain function comes from various sources. Tumors and other conditions in specific parts of the brain cause certain changes in behavior and personality; animal experiments are another major source. This stereotaxic apparatus was used from 1905 in experiments to position needles inside the head of an animal. Similar techniques were first used on humans in 1947. Experiments on animals may be distasteful to some people. Supporters of experimentation claim they have been vital in saving human lives, relieving suffering, and devising new treatments.

HOLDING STILL
Operations on the brain and nerves are some of the most difficult and delicate of all surgery. Here the patient's head is stabilized by a modern stereotaxic apparatus as it is being scanned. The rest of the patient's body is wrapped in metallic foil to keep out radiation.

ECT headset

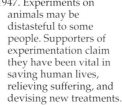

Needle holder

Electrodes for applying electrical current to head

Side-to-side adjustments

Front-to-back adjustments

Width scale

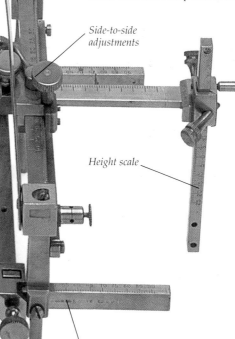

Rods inserted into ears

Side-to-side adjustments

Height scale

Depth scale

The rise of surgery

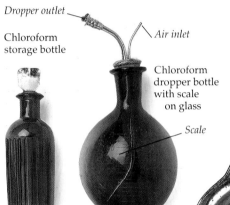

HILARIOUS PARTIES
In the early 19th century, people got intoxicated at "laughing gas parties" and "ether parties." Both substances were used by showmen on their audiences, with entertaining results. Surgical anesthesia arose from these beginnings.

IN THE PAST, MANY PATIENTS UNDERGOING SURGERY were fully awake, writhing in agony as the surgeon – who did not wash his hands – tried to make incisions and finish treatment before the patient died from blood loss. Death due to infection in the wounds was also common. It was not until the 19th century that safe surgery began to develop – Joseph Lister (1827-1912) introduced the use of antiseptics, which prevented infection by killing germs in the wound, and anesthesia was developed, freeing the patient from pain and giving the surgeon more time to operate. An American dentist, Horace Wells (1815-1848), used nitrous oxide as an anesthetic in 1844-1845. Then Thomas Morton (1819-1868), working at Harvard, tried ether, which lasted for longer periods. In October 1846, at the Massachusetts General Hospital, he anesthetized a patient to remove a growth on the neck. So began the modern era of anesthesiology. Within months, various gases and inhalers were being used across North America and Europe to make patients sleep during surgery.

Dropper outlet

Chloroform storage bottle

Air inlet

Chloroform dropper bottle with scale on glass

Scale

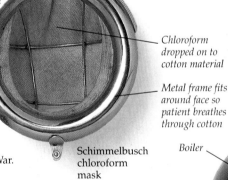

Chloroform dropped on to cotton material

Metal frame fits around face so patient breathes through cotton

Schimmelbusch chloroform mask

FROM ETHER TO CHLOROFORM
Ether was a great improvement on nothing but was unpredictable and had unpleasant effects. In January 1847 James Simpson (1811-1870) of Edinburgh used chloroform gas to ease childbirth pain. In November he tried it for general surgery. In Europe it replaced ether within weeks, with new inhaler and mask designs to give controlled amounts. The Schimmelbusch mask was a common design and used in the First World War.

A BRILLIANT INNOVATOR
Joseph Lister introduced antiseptics, said to have "saved more lives than all the wars of history [have] thrown away." He also developed other practices still used today, such as using catgut to tie off blood vessels.

Steam nozzle

Carbolic nozzle

Carbolic tube

Boiler

Insulated handle

Cage around flame heat source

THE CARBOLIC STEAM SPRAY
In 1865, following Pasteur's work on the germ theory (p. 32 and p. 35), Lister began to practice antisepsis – using chemicals to kill germs in and around wounds. By 1870 he had developed an antiseptic carbolic acid spray to destroy germs in the air. Many doctors opposed Lister's ideas – some still held Galen's view that pus was "laudable": a septic wound showed that an unwanted humor (p. 19) was coming out of the body. But opposition faded after Lister successfully lanced an abscess for Queen Victoria. Using antisepsis, death rates in Lister's surgery fell from about 50 to 5 percent in two years. But gradually antiseptic methods gave way to asepsis (p. 49).

Carbolic jar

ANTISEPSIS TO ASEPSIS

Following Lister's lead, researchers explored other antiseptic chemicals and machines, as shown below. But operating in a chemical mist was unpleasant, and research showed that germs in the wound, on skin, and on equipment were more dangerous than those in the air. In the 1890s asepsis – preventing germs from getting into the wound by sterilizing clothes, equipment, and other germ-carrying objects – took over from antisepsis.

Winding handle for clockwork motor

Clockwork motor

Hammer to tap dry medicament container

Spray outlet

Hammer-action antiseptic spray (1879)

Dry medicaments are put in here if required

Air inlet with fan inside

Antiseptic-soaked gauze inside here

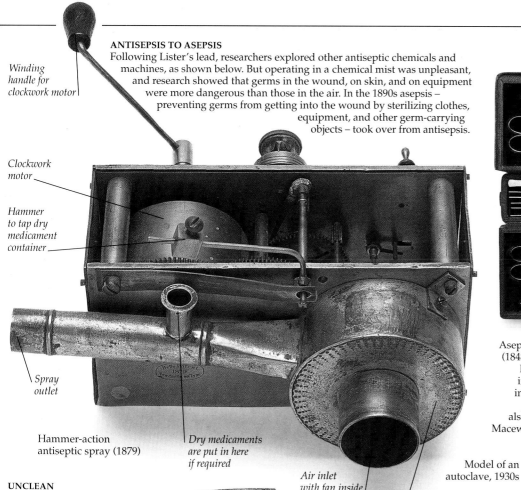

Surgical set *c.* 1870

STERILIZATION SETS

Asepsis was pioneered by Sir William Macewen (1848-1924), successor to Lister at Glasgow, and Ernst von Bergmann (1836-1907), a surgeon in Berlin. As it became widespread, surgical instruments were made of steel to withstand high-temperature sterilization. Both men also introduced new techniques. In particular, Macewen pioneered the removal of brain tumors.

Model of an autoclave, 1930s

Lid

Sterilizing compartment

Boiler

Tray for instruments

UNCLEAN OPERATIONS

This 19th-century engraving shows a patient under anesthetic, with a mask held over his face, being prepared for surgery. An audience of students and observers watches, in what is literally an "operating theater." The surgeons and assistants, who are all male, wear clean clothes mainly to look smart; the equipment on the table is not sterilized.

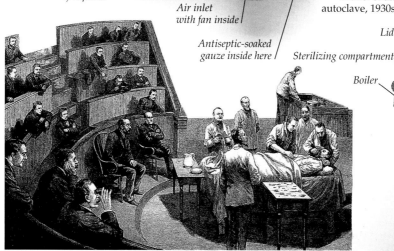

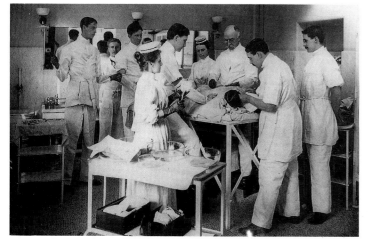

CLEAN AND WHITE

By 1900, conditions had changed. Some surgeons and staff, like these in New York, wore white to show up dirt; instruments were sterilized and covered; and the theater was easy to clean with antiseptics. Female nurses had become an integral part of the team. These surgeons are led by Charles McBurney (1845-1913), a pioneer in anesthetics and appendectomy (appendix removal).

STERILIZATION AND PROGRESS

Machines called autoclaves were invented in the 1880s to sterilize instruments with high-pressure, superheated steam. Surgical instruments became nickel- or chrome-plated for easier cleaning and longer life. With better anesthesia, patients could be kept unconscious and still for longer periods; with better asepsis, risks of postoperative infection lessened. Surgeons could examine parts of the body they had largely ignored, and were attempting longer, more delicate procedures.

Under the knife

REPLACING BLOOD
This First World War blood transfusion kit has connecting tubes, a glass storage jar, and hollow needles and tubes for bleeding the donor and introducing blood into the patient. Blood treated with anticoagulants, which prevent the blood from clotting (forming into lumps), was first stored with some success during this war.

THE ADVANCES IN ANESTHESIA, antisepsis-asepsis, and X-rays (pp. 48-49 and p. 38) meant that, by 1900, surgeons were developing a variety of new operations, techniques, and equipment to save lives and relieve suffering. But one restriction was blood loss. If a patient bled too much, life was endangered. Blood transfusions – substituting blood donated by other people – were unpredictable and sometimes fatal. In the early 1900s, the Austrian medical researcher Karl Landsteiner (1868-1943) tested many blood samples and discovered that not all blood was the same. He unraveled the intricacies of the ABO blood group system, thereby making transfusions much safer. Then in 1939 Landsteiner helped to identify Rhesus, another blood group system. At once the information was used in the first aid stations and field hospitals of the Second World War, and thousands of lives were saved with antibiotics (p. 42). Yet despite these advances, the surgeon's basic tools would still be recognized by a surgeon from ancient Greece or Rome (p. 19).

BLOOD FROM THE BANK
Until the 1930s, most blood transfusions were arranged with a selected donor – usually a relative of the patient – and with the blood still warm. Since the Second World War, methods were developed to filter blood, treat it with chemicals to increase its shelf life, separate it into its various components, and refrigerate it. Blood banks now provide vast quantities of blood products for routine surgery and emergencies. But supplies are rarely adequate, and new donors are always needed.

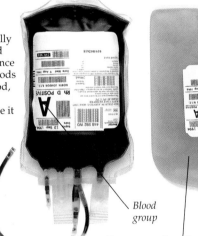

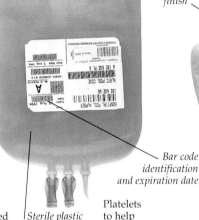

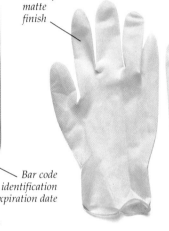

Antislip matte finish

Blood group

Concentrated red blood cells

Sterile plastic bag container

Platelets to help blood clot

Bar code identification and expiration date

SURGICAL GLOVES
In 1890, the American surgeon William Halsted (1852-1922) asked the Goodyear Rubber Company to make some thin rubber gloves to protect nurses' hands against mercuric chloride sterilizing solution. Soon all surgeons and their staff were wearing them. Halsted, a brilliant but cautious operator, became addicted in the mid 1880s to cocaine (and later morphine), after investigating its pain-killing effects.

Extremely sharp disposable stainless steel blade

INCISION
Amid the space-age technology of the operating room, simple instruments are still vital. The ultra-sharp scalpel, used for incision, has been around for at least 5,000 years. Some had decorative handles of bone or ivory, but high-temperature sterilization required all-metal versions by the 1880s. The detachable disposable blade arrived in 1925.

Ridged handle for secure pen-grip

Scalpel

Retractor

Shoulder for grip when pulling

RETRACTION
The body's skin and superficial tissues are elastic and will spring back after the scalpel's initial incisions. Retractors have hooked ends to hold the tissues apart and allow a larger viewing and working area. The hooks come in different sizes.

Blunt hook

PROBING TISSUES
The muscles and main parts of the body are not attached tightly to each other. With some probing and teasing, they can be separated, rather like easing pieces of fruit out of jelly. The probe is a narrow, blunt device used for this purpose. The Volkmann spoon design, with two small cup-shaped ends, is named after the eminent German surgeon Richard von Volkmann (1830-1889).

Narrow neck for probing into confined spaces

Cup-shaped end

Volkmann spoon

Ridged finger grip

Cup-shaped end

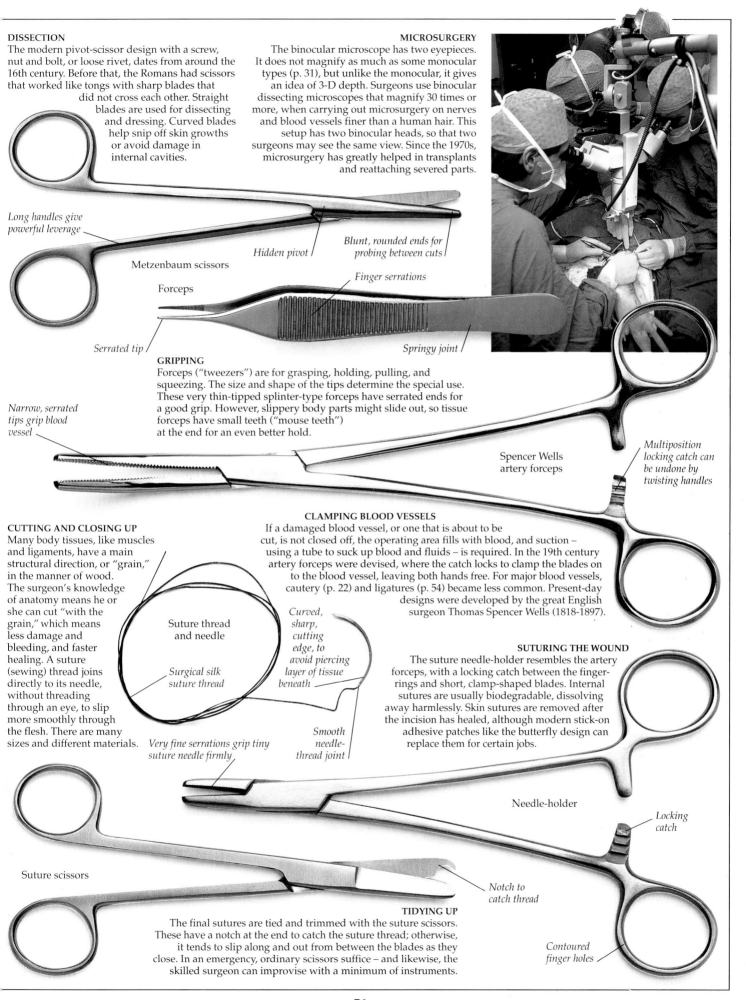

DISSECTION

The modern pivot-scissor design with a screw, nut and bolt, or loose rivet, dates from around the 16th century. Before that, the Romans had scissors that worked like tongs with sharp blades that did not cross each other. Straight blades are used for dissecting and dressing. Curved blades help snip off skin growths or avoid damage in internal cavities.

Long handles give powerful leverage

Metzenbaum scissors

Hidden pivot

Blunt, rounded ends for probing between cuts

Forceps

Finger serrations

Serrated tip

Springy joint

MICROSURGERY

The binocular microscope has two eyepieces. It does not magnify as much as some monocular types (p. 31), but unlike the monocular, it gives an idea of 3-D depth. Surgeons use binocular dissecting microscopes that magnify 30 times or more, when carrying out microsurgery on nerves and blood vessels finer than a human hair. This setup has two binocular heads, so that two surgeons may see the same view. Since the 1970s, microsurgery has greatly helped in transplants and reattaching severed parts.

GRIPPING

Forceps ("tweezers") are for grasping, holding, pulling, and squeezing. The size and shape of the tips determine the special use. These very thin-tipped splinter-type forceps have serrated ends for a good grip. However, slippery body parts might slide out, so tissue forceps have small teeth ("mouse teeth") at the end for an even better hold.

Narrow, serrated tips grip blood vessel

Spencer Wells artery forceps

Multiposition locking catch can be undone by twisting handles

CUTTING AND CLOSING UP

Many body tissues, like muscles and ligaments, have a main structural direction, or "grain," in the manner of wood. The surgeon's knowledge of anatomy means he or she can cut "with the grain," which means less damage and bleeding, and faster healing. A suture (sewing) thread joins directly to its needle, without threading through an eye, to slip more smoothly through the flesh. There are many sizes and different materials.

Suture thread and needle

Surgical silk suture thread

Curved, sharp, cutting edge, to avoid piercing layer of tissue beneath

Very fine serrations grip tiny suture needle firmly

Smooth needle-thread joint

CLAMPING BLOOD VESSELS

If a damaged blood vessel, or one that is about to be cut, is not closed off, the operating area fills with blood, and suction – using a tube to suck up blood and fluids – is required. In the 19th century artery forceps were devised, where the catch locks to clamp the blades on to the blood vessel, leaving both hands free. For major blood vessels, cautery (p. 22) and ligatures (p. 54) became less common. Present-day designs were developed by the great English surgeon Thomas Spencer Wells (1818-1897).

SUTURING THE WOUND

The suture needle-holder resembles the artery forceps, with a locking catch between the finger-rings and short, clamp-shaped blades. Internal sutures are usually biodegradable, dissolving away harmlessly. Skin sutures are removed after the incision has healed, although modern stick-on adhesive patches like the butterfly design can replace them for certain jobs.

Needle-holder

Locking catch

Suture scissors

Notch to catch thread

TIDYING UP

The final sutures are tied and trimmed with the suture scissors. These have a notch at the end to catch the suture thread; otherwise, it tends to slip along and out from between the blades as they close. In an emergency, ordinary scissors suffice – and likewise, the skilled surgeon can improvise with a minimum of instruments.

Contoured finger holes

Revolutionary technology

As MEDICAL EXPERTISE continues to grow, a greater number of diseases can be treated and increasingly more complicated surgery can be performed, using some of the world's most advanced technology. One of the newest trends in surgery is toward minimally invasive surgery, a phrase that came to prominence in 1985. It means "invading" the patient's body less, by making the smallest possible cuts and doing the least possible damage to body tissues. This lessens the trauma (damage) that occurs in open surgery. Trauma takes longer to heal and has greater risks of complication. There are three important areas of advance. First is in X-rays and scanners (pp. 38-39), mainly for visualizing the inside of the body; second is the replacement of scalpels and some forms of cautery by the precise, controllable energy of the laser beam. Third is the new generation of endoscopes (pp. 28-29) that incorporates fiber optics and lasers for peering through "keyhole" incisions in the body and for carrying out treatments.

Laser tube

THE LASER SCALPEL
The laser was invented as a working device in 1960. Its intense, concentrated, purified light affects body tissues in various ways, depending on the type of laser and the amount of energy in the beam. One of the first uses was to "melt away" a type of birthmark called a port-wine stain. High-power cutting lasers can slice like the sharpest scalpel. They can be controlled with great precision, cause less pain, and heat-weld tiny blood vessels shut as they go, thereby reducing bleeding. The beams shine from swan-necked tubes so that they can "cut around corners."

0.45 mm working channel attachments

Fiber optic can be retracted while going through bone, to avoid damage

900 mm insert portion can be steered around corners

THE MICRO-ENDOSCOPE
The part of this endoscope that is inserted into the body is less than 3 mm in diameter, yet houses six channels. The main working channel is 1.1 mm in diameter and can be used in various ways, for example as a tunnel for a minute biopsy forceps to remove a sample of tissue, or for laser fibers to treat tissues. Two 0.45 mm working channels suck in air, flush fluid, or pump drug solutions. Two 0.5 mm channels carry light, and the fiber-optic channel houses a 10,000-strand bundle to convey an image back out (see opposite).

1.1 mm working channel attachment

Rounded tip has openings of six channels and is radio-opaque (visible on X-ray)

Hand-held eyepiece to see view conveyed by fiber-optic bundle

Illumination channels connected to halogen or xenon light source

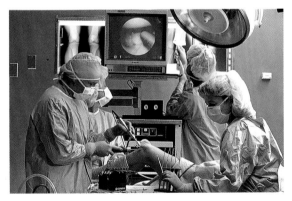

INSIDE THE KNEE
The arthroscope is an endoscope designed to look inside joints such as the knee, which may become twisted and damaged in various sports. The scope is inserted into a tiny slit in the skin, and through the natural spaces between the muscles, ligaments, and tendons, so that the inner structure of the joint can be lit by bright light and visualized on the monitor screen. After diagnosis, keyhole surgery can be carried out using the same route.

THE CARDIAC CATHETER
A catheter is a long, slender, flexible tube that is inserted into the body for a variety of purposes. If it is made of a suitable radio-opaque material (visible on X-ray), the catheter can be seen on screen and steered along blood vessels or between organs. This catheter was inserted into an arm vein and steered to the heart, to measure the blood pressure inside the heart by a micromechanical pressure sensor in its tip. Similar catheters can take blood samples or take tiny pieces of tissue for biopsy (analysis).

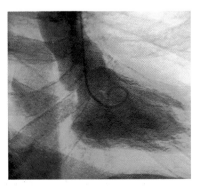

FIBER-OPTIC ENDOSCOPES

The first working endoscopes to be inserted into the body – rigid tubes with mirrors and glass lenses – were devised in the 1850s to look up the urethra into the bladder. In the 1950s flexible bundles of optical fibers were developed. These carry light to the endoscope tip to illuminate the inside of the body cavity and convey what it looks like. Each strand in the bundle relays a piece of the view, like a mosaic, so the surgeon can monitor the scope's progress on a monitor, as shown below. The endoscope is flexible and can be steered up/down and left/right as it passes into the body. Micro-endoscopes go up the nose into the sinus air spaces; via the back of the throat and eustachian tube into the ear; along blood vessels into the heart; down the digestive tract to the liver and gall bladder; and up the urinary tract to the kidneys.

LASER THERAPY

Low-power lasers are now used for many types of treatments. At relatively higher intensities they can weld together tissues or blood vessels, seal small ulcers, and obliterate unwanted tissues such as atherosclerotic plaques (fatty lumps that may block arteries) and tumors. At lower intensities (less than 500 mW), when treating the skin and body surfaces, they help relieve pain, treat skeletal and muscular injuries, and treat skin conditions, such as burns, eczema, psoriasis, and ulcers.

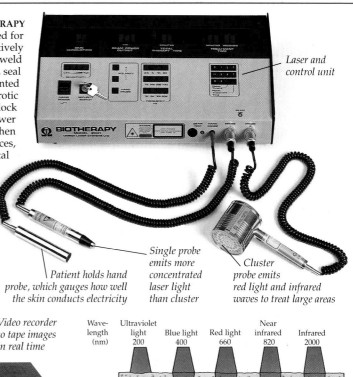

Laser and control unit

Patient holds hand probe, which gauges how well the skin conducts electricity

Single probe emits more concentrated laser light than cluster

Cluster probe emits red light and infrared waves to treat large areas

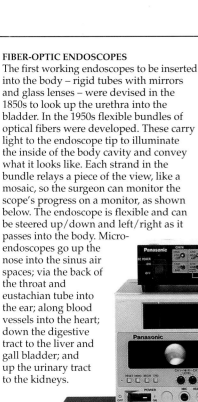

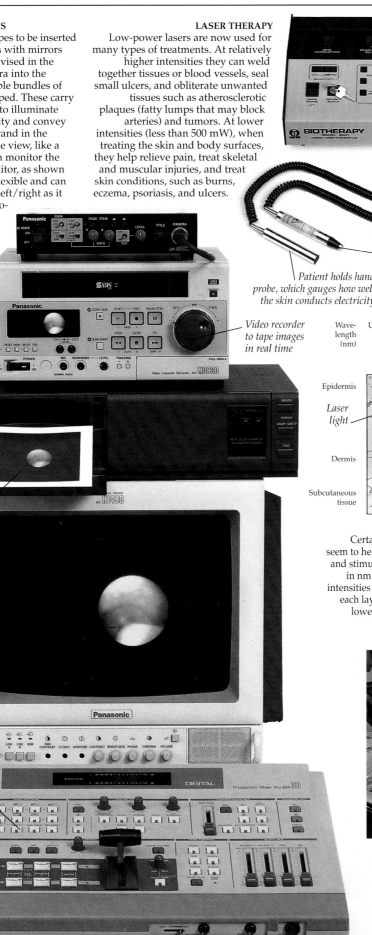

Video recorder to tape images in real time

Photographic printer for selected still images

High-resolution monitor gives very detailed picture

Vision mixer can place other images on screen, for comparison and super-imposition

| Wave-length (nm) | Ultraviolet light 200 | Blue light 400 | Red light 660 | Near infrared 820 | Infrared 2000 |

Epidermis

Laser light

Dermis

Subcutaneous tissue

LIGHT RELIEF

Certain wavelengths of light, especially infrared waves, seem to help relieve pain, kill infection, reduce inflammation, and stimulate healing. The different wavelengths (measured in nm – billionths of a meter) are produced at controlled intensities emitted by a laser unit. These penetrate safely into each layer of skin – from the tough outer epidermis, to the lower dermis with its blood vessels and touch-sensitive endings, to the subcutaneous fatty tissue below.

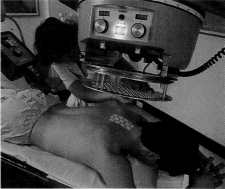

RADIOTHERAPY

Radiation ("rays") from X-ray and similar machines can be carefully controlled and focused to destroy unwanted cells, growths, and tumors. This is termed radiotherapy. In gamma radiotherapy, shown here, the radiation is in the form of gamma rays from a radioactive form of the metal cobalt. In some cases a small capsule of radioactive material is implanted into the body temporarily.

Artificial parts

AN IMPLANT IS AN INTERNAL artificial device made to take over the function of a body part. A transplant is a living organ (usually human, sometimes from a pig or other animal) that is put into a patient. A prosthesis is an artificial external body part. Transplants and implants are modern innovations, but removing parts (amputation) has taken place for centuries. In the 16th century Ambroise Paré (1510-1590), a French army doctor, improved his own survival rates by reintroducing the Roman technique of tying off blood vessels during amputation to reduce blood loss. He also dressed wounds with clean bandages and ointments (including one made from eggs, oil of roses, and turpentine), rather than cauterizing them or sealing them with boiling oil. However, it was not until the use of antisepsis and asepsis (pp. 48-49) in the late 19th century that survival rates improved greatly. With the mechanical and electrical advances of the 19th and 20th centuries, prostheses, which were usually made of wood or metal, have also much improved.

CAPTAIN HOOK
In the novel *Peter Pan* by J. M. Barrie, published in 1904, the pirate Captain Hook is named after the hook that is in place of his hand, which was bitten off by a crocodile. People often wore practical spare parts to help them in their jobs and daily life.

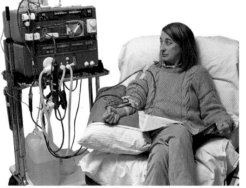

KIDNEY DIALYSIS
The kidneys filter blood and remove wastes and excess water. If they do not work well, a renal dialyzer, or "artificial kidney," may be used. The patient is connected to the machine, and the blood is filtered through membranes and tubes and returned to the body. Dialyzers were first developed in the 1940s, using sausage skins as membranes. Dialysis is usually done for several hours, several times a week. Automated machines were introduced for home use in the early 1960s.

Valve open – ball away from ring | Valve shut – blood flows back and presses ball against ring

INSIDE THE HEART
Throughout a person's life, the heart's valves open and shut more than once every second. In some people the valves are malformed or weakened by infection (bacterial endocarditis), so they work less efficiently. Artificial heart valves, such the Starr-Edwards ball-and-cage design above, can replace the natural ones for years.

PACING THE HEART
The heart's own "pacemaker" sends electric pulses through its muscle to make it beat. But sometimes it beats too fast, too slow, or is uncoordinated. The electronic pacemaker, first implanted in 1960, is placed near the heart and produces regular signals. In 1973 new, longer-lasting lithium batteries were introduced. Computerized programmable pacemakers were developed in the 1980s.

Battery | Plastic case | Electric circuit provides timed pulse of electricity

Rigid thumb riveted in place

Pivot joint for pair of fingers

Attachment to leather strap on stump

MECHANICAL HAND
Paré designed artificial hands and limbs for his amputation patients. This 17th-century iron hand and wrist looked realistic under a glove. The two pairs of fingers could be moved at the joints to do simple hooking-type tasks.

REALISM AND FUNCTION
Some replacement limbs were exquisitely crafted from valuable leathers, ivory, and precious metals; others were simply carved out of wood. This 1908 arm was made for a young patient born without forearm or hand. (At the time, spare parts for children were rare, since they were expensive and the child soon outgrew them.) Each part is designed for comfort and to make the best use of the patient's remaining movements and abilities.

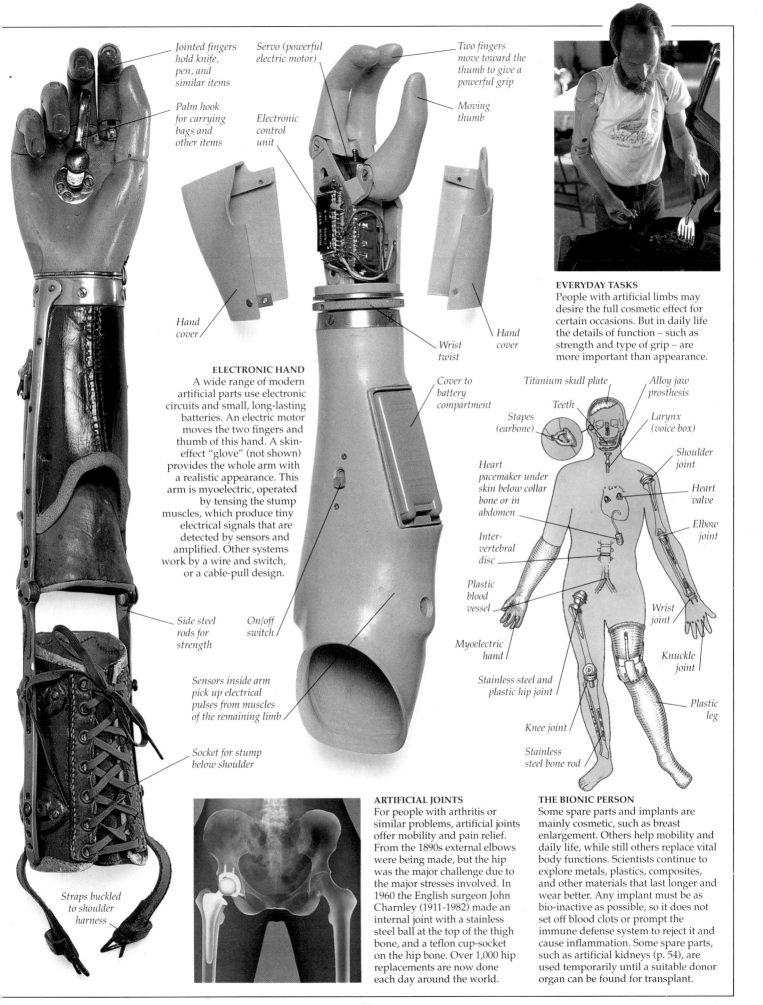

Jointed fingers
hold knife,
pen, and
similar items

Servo (powerful
electric motor)

Two fingers
move toward the
thumb to give a
powerful grip

Moving
thumb

Palm hook
for carrying
bags and
other items

Electronic
control
unit

Hand
cover

Hand
cover

Wrist
twist

EVERYDAY TASKS
People with artificial limbs may
desire the full cosmetic effect for
certain occasions. But in daily life
the details of function – such as
strength and type of grip – are
more important than appearance.

ELECTRONIC HAND
A wide range of modern
artificial parts use electronic
circuits and small, long-lasting
batteries. An electric motor
moves the two fingers and
thumb of this hand. A skin-
effect "glove" (not shown)
provides the whole arm with
a realistic appearance. This
arm is myoelectric, operated
by tensing the stump
muscles, which produce tiny
electrical signals that are
detected by sensors and
amplified. Other systems
work by a wire and switch,
or a cable-pull design.

Cover to
battery
compartment

Titanium skull plate

Teeth

Alloy jaw
prosthesis

Stapes
(earbone)

Larynx
(voice box)

Shoulder
joint

Heart
pacemaker under
skin below collar
bone or in
abdomen

Heart
valve

Inter-
vertebral
disc

Elbow
joint

Plastic
blood
vessel

Wrist
joint

Myoelectric
hand

Knuckle
joint

Side steel
rods for
strength

On/off
switch

Stainless steel and
plastic hip joint

Plastic
leg

Knee joint

Sensors inside arm
pick up electrical
pulses from muscles
of the remaining limb

Stainless
steel bone rod

Socket for stump
below shoulder

Straps buckled
to shoulder
harness

ARTIFICIAL JOINTS
For people with arthritis or
similar problems, artificial joints
offer mobility and pain relief.
From the 1890s external elbows
were being made, but the hip
was the major challenge due to
the major stresses involved. In
1960 the English surgeon John
Charnley (1911-1982) made an
internal joint with a stainless
steel ball at the top of the thigh
bone, and a teflon cup-socket
on the hip bone. Over 1,000 hip
replacements are now done
each day around the world.

THE BIONIC PERSON
Some spare parts and implants are
mainly cosmetic, such as breast
enlargement. Others help mobility and
daily life, while still others replace vital
body functions. Scientists continue to
explore metals, plastics, composites,
and other materials that last longer and
wear better. Any implant must be as
bio-inactive as possible, so it does not
set off blood clots or prompt the
immune defense system to reject it and
cause inflammation. Some spare parts,
such as artificial kidneys (p. 54), are
used temporarily until a suitable donor
organ can be found for transplant.

Caring for the sick

THE RISE OF NURSING as a highly trained profession is closely linked with the changing roles of men and women in medicine. Some 2,000 years ago, wounded Roman soldiers were cared for by auxiliary soldiers and slaves. With the spread of Christianity, monks and nuns cared for the sick. Until the 14th century, women could generally practice medicine, and a few became highly respected physicians and midwives. But then physicians and surgeons organized themselves into male-dominated institutions, and women were rarely licensed to practice medicine. Most nursing took place at home and was haphazard. In the 18th and 19th centuries, public hospitals were built, but even then the nurses were mostly untrained, poorly paid women. Catholic and Protestant groups began to train nurses, and in 1836 a priest, Theodor Fliedner (1800-1864), and his wife founded a three-year training course for nurse-deaconesses in Germany. Prison reformer Elizabeth Fry (1780-1845) visited them and, back in England, helped found the Institute of Nursing, which improved standards. But it was Florence Nightingale (1820-1910) who revolutionized standards of cleanliness and patient care, and brought nursing into the modern age.

CONVENTIONAL NURSING
For centuries religious orders have followed their vows of charity by looking after the ill and infirm, and providing them with food and drink, beds, bedding, and clothes. The nursing term "sister" derives from the sisters of the convent or nunnery. However, the medical licensing system limited to what extent nurses could give medicines.

Spout for drinking

POSSET
Posset was an easily digested, nourishing drink or soup based on hot milk curdled with ales or beers, and flavored with herbs and spices such as ginger and cinnamon. It was used as a remedy for colds and other minor ailments. As nursing moved from the duties of wife or female relative at home into a fully fledged hospital profession, the posset pot spread on to the wards. Other items that originated in domestic settings also became standard hospital equipment, such as bedpans, back rests, and leg frames, to hold the weight of bedclothes off the feet of gout sufferers.

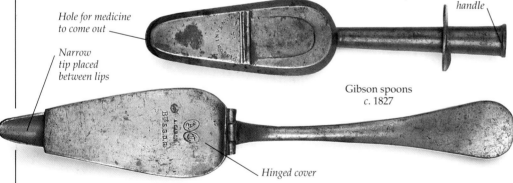

Hole for medicine to come out

Narrow tip placed between lips

Medicine poured into hollow handle

Gibson spoons
c. 1827

Hinged cover

TAKING MEDICINE
Most sick people take their medicine dutifully. But children and the mentally ill may refuse to swallow. In 1827 Englishman Charles Gibson designed spoons with lids to prevent spillage and ensure the contents went down the patient's throat – even by forceful persuasion.

"THE LADY WITH THE LAMP"
Florence Nightingale came from a well-to-do family, but she decided to devote her life to nursing. She read widely about health matters and made contacts in the medical establishment. In 1853 Britain entered the Crimea War; casualties were horrific. In November 1854 Florence Nightingale took 38 nurses to Scutari's dark, dirty, rat-infested Barrack Hospital. In a few months it was bright and clean, and a patient's chance of dying had fallen from almost 1 in 3 to nearer 1 in 40. In 1856 she returned to England and began to train training matrons; that is, to teach senior nurses how to teach nursing. Many Nightingale Schools were set up, and her book *Notes on Nursing* (1859) was the profession's first bestseller. Florence Nightingale believed that, "Nursing . . . ought to signify the proper use of fresh air, light, warmth, cleanliness, quiet . . . and diet".

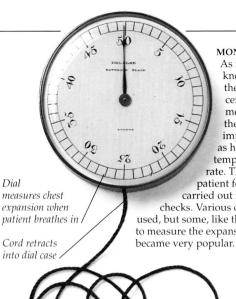

Dial measures chest expansion when patient breathes in

Cord retracts into dial case

Cord placed around patient's chest

MONITORING PATIENTS

As nurses became more knowledgeable during the latter half of the 19th century, they administered medicines prescribed by the doctor and measured important features such as heartbeat (pulse), body temperature, and breathing rate. They also observed the patient for signs of illness, and carried out regular around-the-clock checks. Various diagnostic devices were used, but some, like the stethometer, a device to measure the expansion of the chest, never became very popular.

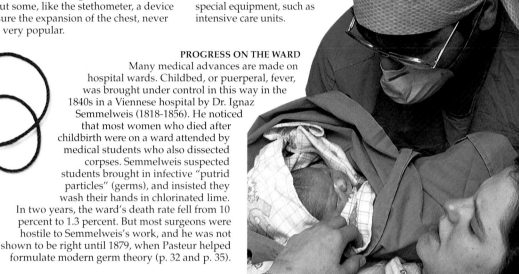

Mercury in bulb

Scale for measuring temperature

NURSING SKILLS

The clinical thermometer was recognized as an important diagnostic tool by about 1880. But it was (and still is) a delicate device, which can give inaccurate readings if not used correctly. Nurses are trained in the correct and safe use of this and hundreds of other health-care items. As nursing became more sophisticated and complicated from the 1950s, it began to divide into specialties. Some nurses specialize in working with children, the elderly, specific groups of diseases such as cancers, or with special equipment, such as intensive care units.

PROGRESS ON THE WARD

Many medical advances are made on hospital wards. Childbed, or puerperal, fever, was brought under control in this way in the 1840s in a Viennese hospital by Dr. Ignaz Semmelweis (1818-1856). He noticed that most women who died after childbirth were on a ward attended by medical students who also dissected corpses. Semmelweis suspected students brought in infective "putrid particles" (germs), and insisted they wash their hands in chlorinated lime. In two years, the ward's death rate fell from 10 percent to 1.3 percent. But most surgeons were hostile to Semmelweis's work, and he was not shown to be right until 1879, when Pasteur helped formulate modern germ theory (p. 32 and p. 35).

Caring for newborn babies

Caring for ill newborn babies is a very specialized task. The "neonatal intensive care unit" is now known by more user-friendly names, such as "intensive care baby unit" (ICBU). It has a seemingly baffling array of incubators, pipes, tubes, gadgets, and monitor screens. Yet the tiny patients still need large doses of tender loving care.

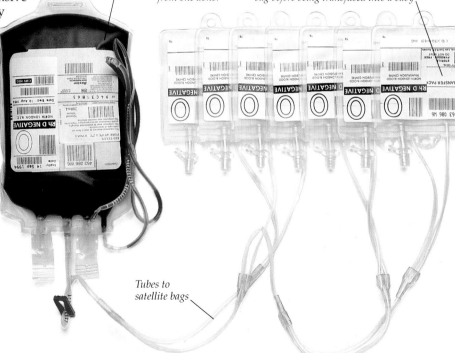

Main 280-milliliter bag of red blood cells from one donor

Small samples of blood drawn into satellite bag before being transfused into a baby

Tubes to satellite bags

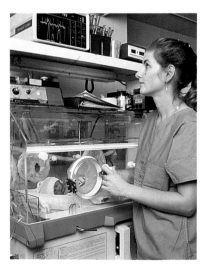

SPECIALIZING IN SMALL PATIENT CARE

Highly trained nurses in the ICBU or SCBU (Special Care Baby Unit) carry out some of the work formerly done by doctors, allowing doctors to make full use of their own training. Nurses are also skilled at coping with distressed patients and distraught relatives, often in extremely stressful situations.

BLOOD TRANSFUSIONS FOR BABIES

Tiny, premature babies are quite likely to need a blood transfusion. In fact, some may need 10 or more. Each involves just 1-2 teaspoons of blood. This blood bag is designed specifically for babies. It has seven "satellite" bags, each containing the right amount of blood for one transfusion. This means that blood is not wasted and a baby can receive blood from just one or two donors, which reduces the risk of infections.

Emergency treatment

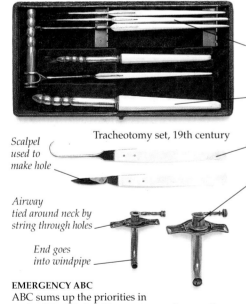

PUMPING OUT POISONS
If poisonous substances are swallowed, prompt pumping of the stomach contents can stop them from being absorbed into the bloodstream and causing further damage. Nowadays patients can take medicine and water to make them vomit.

THE IDEA OF EMERGENCY treatment for urgent, even life-threatening illness has changed through the centuries. In ancient times, unless a physician was within shouting distance, bystanders did the best they could. Urgency in medicine remained a common but unpredictable event for centuries. Like many medical advances, the first organized use of ambulances came about during wartime. In about 1796, during Napoleon's invasion of Italy, the French military surgeon Dominique Jean Larrey (1766-1842) introduced "flying ambulances," light, fast, one-horse vehicles for removing the wounded from the battlefront and taking them to a hospital station to be treated. In America, the Civil War (1861-1865) raged for two years before "ambulance trains" of horse-drawn wagons (like the Wild West wagon trains) were organized in 1863. Today, telephones and radios are used to call help, and fast ambulances and helicopters are sent to the patient. Highly trained paramedics are ready to begin life-saving treatment within seconds, using a wide array of drugs and equipment. Expectations have also changed. Patients can now hope to survive many events that would almost certainly have proved fatal 50 years ago.

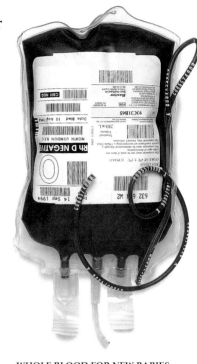

WHOLE BLOOD FOR NEW BABIES
Blood banks carry various types and components of blood, many of which are used in routine operations (p. 50). But some are designed specifically for emergency use. This whole-blood preparation can save a baby's life. It is given, if necessary, to babies whose mothers have Rhesus D negative blood. Due to immune reactions in the mother's body, the baby's blood can be damaged during pregnancy, so at birth it requires a complete blood exchange.

Scalpels and needles

Bougie enlarges hole

Tracheotomy set, 19th century

Scalpel used to make hole

Retractor used with scalpel to make hole

Breathing tubes can be attached here

Airway tied around neck by string through holes

End goes into windpipe

EMERGENCY ABC
ABC sums up the priorities in saving life. A is for Airway: ensure the mouth, throat, and windpipe are clear. B is for Breathing: check that air is being drawn into the lungs. C is for Circulation: is the heart beating to circulate vital oxygen-carrying blood around the body? If the mouth or throat is blocked (stage A), it may be vital to make a hole in the lower neck into the windpipe. A pen lid may suffice, but a tracheotomy set does minimal damage.

SLOWING BLOOD LOSS
So much blood may be lost from a large wound, especially if an artery is severed, that the patient may collapse and die. Also, any open wound may become infected. Bleeding should be controlled by applying direct pressure to the wound, then bandaging it to slow blood loss and keep out germs. Pressure stops the immediate blood flow, and the body's blood-clotting mechanisms start to work. The wound is then cleaned, sewn up (blood vessels tied, if necessary), and dressed.

Bandage to secure pads and protect wound from bumps and further contamination

First pad to soak up blood

Pressure to keep wound closed

Second pad applied over first to absorb blood

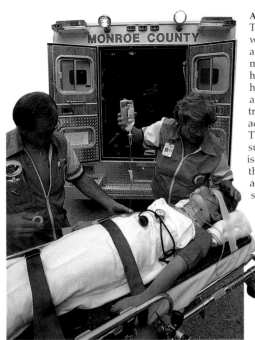

AMBULANCE EQUIPMENT

Today's ambulance bristles with emergency equipment and hi-tech aids to deal with medical emergencies, such as heart attacks and cerebral hemorrhages (bleeding in or around the brain), as well as trauma (injury) victims after accidents and woundings. This casualty has cuts and a suspected spinal injury, so he is strapped to the stretcher at the body and forehead, using a preformed plastic collar to stabilize his neck movements. The ambulance staff keeps a close watch on breathing, using a face mask to give extra oxygen (see below) and replace lost body fluids from the bottle of saline (salt) solution. A needle is put into the patient's arm and the solution seeps into the vein.

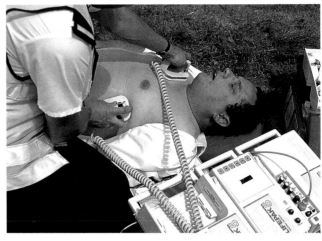

THE DEFIBRILLATOR

If the heart stops, blood ceases to circulate around the body. Within minutes, cells and tissues start to die – especially in the brain. The defibrillator is designed to "shock" a stopped, or fibrillating, heart back into a regular beat, by passing a burst of electricity between electrodes placed on the chest.

EMERGENCY HOSPITAL EQUIPMENT

The crash cart is immediately available in hospitals to deal with a variety of emergency situations and illnesses, from cardiac arrest (absence of heartbeat) to intense allergic reaction to a drug. The items are designed to revive the patient and support life processes until the patient can receive more specialized treatment. Instead of breathing air, of which only one-fifth is vital oxygen, the patient can breathe pure oxygen from the gas cylinder. In cases of severe facial injuries, the patient may need an airway in the nose or mouth, down into the throat. Each item is in a standard position on the cart so it is easily found.

Drawer containing oxygen mask, color-coded green tubing, airways, and tubes

Drawer containing items such as syringes, needles, dressings, scalpels, sutures, suture scissors, and long needles for injecting directly into the heart

Fluid products, tubing, and needles for "drips" (intravenous [in-the-vein] infusions)

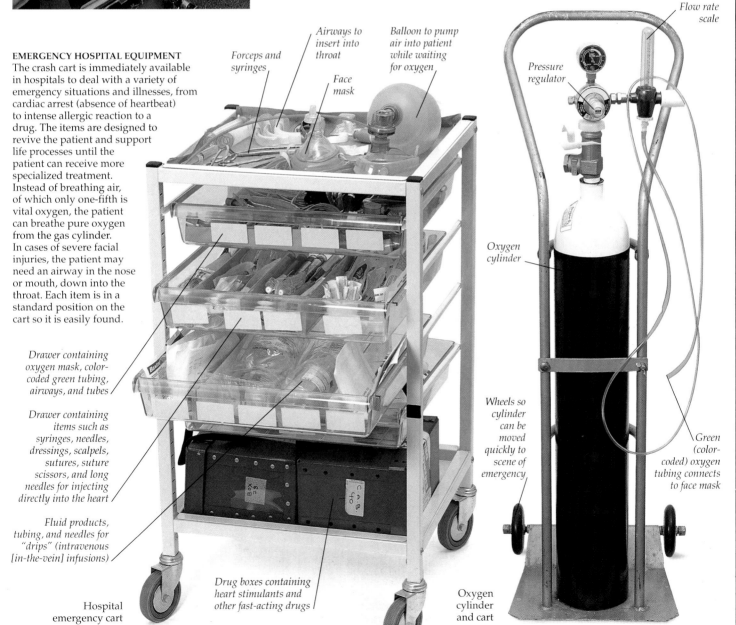

Forceps and syringes

Airways to insert into throat

Balloon to pump air into patient while waiting for oxygen

Face mask

Flow rate scale

Pressure regulator

Oxygen cylinder

Wheels so cylinder can be moved quickly to scene of emergency

Green (color-coded) oxygen tubing connects to face mask

Hospital emergency cart

Drug boxes containing heart stimulants and other fast-acting drugs

Oxygen cylinder and cart

General practice

In MANY COUNTRIES, family doctors are the first stop in the medical care system for those who are ill (or think they are ill). They are termed primary-care physicians and are trained in a wide range of health and medical matters, although they may also have their own special interests, such as dermatology (skin conditions) or obstetrics (care of pregnant women and unborn babies). The family doctor usually gets to know patients and their families, and can offer advice on staying healthy, on social issues relating to health, and on specific medical matters. The doctor's office is equipped with a range of basic diagnostic tests and equipment for investigating and treating common ailments. Some people have less common conditions that require special diagnosis or treatment, so the doctor refers them to another physician having special training and experience for the disease in question.

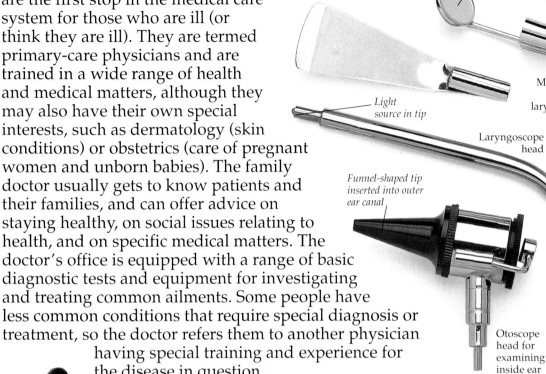

Tongue depressor for laryngoscope

Angled mirror to reflect view

Gap widens to hold nostrils open

Nasal speculum

Screw widens gap

Screws onto otoscope head here

Light source in tip

Mirror head fits over laryngoscope

Rotating set of magnifying lenses for examining the eye

Laryngoscope head

Lens indicator

Funnel-shaped tip inserted into outer ear canal

Otoscope head for examining inside ear

Various head attachments screw on here

Ophthalmoscope

TO THE HOSPITAL
Most hospitals deal with patients with various medical problems. They have specialists who have trained in specific areas, such as renal medicine (of the kidneys), neurology (conditions of the brain and nerves), or thoracic surgery (of the chest). Obviously life-threatening emergencies must be dealt with at once, so hospitals have emergency rooms, which are specially equiped and staffed to deal with sudden medical situations.

DIAGNOSTIC KIT
Ophthalmoscopes for looking into eyes and otoscopes for ears (p. 28) are important parts of any diagnostic kit. Ear infections, especially common in children, should be treated before they cause longer-term damage and hearing loss. Some apparent learning or speech difficulties result from early loss of hearing. Looking into the eye not only warns of eye problems, but is also a way of viewing living blood vessels directly. This indicates the general health of blood circulation and conditions that affect it, such as diabetes.

Hollow barrel of needle

Guard stops operator's hand sliding on to needle

Handle detached here

Trocar

DRAINING FLUID
The trocar is a large-bore, sharp-tipped, hollow needle, which is slid through the skin and flesh into a cavity where fluid has accumulated in conditions such as water on the knee. It is usually used only if the quantity of fluid is fairly large. If the fluid is needed for diagnosis, it is more usual to drain the fluid with a syringe and a wide-bore needle.

CHECKING THE THROAT
Almost everyone suffers the occasional common cold or sore throat. Sometimes this can be a prelude to something more serious, such as tonsillitis or laryngitis, or very occasionally diphtheria, where a crusty membrane grows on the very inflamed throat and windpipe and may obstruct breathing. To check, the doctor may look down the back of the mouth and into the throat, toward the larynx (voicebox) and windpipe. This long-handled laryngeal mirror reflects the view outward.

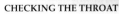

Highly polished metal mirror

Laryngeal mirror

One-piece sterilizable steel construction

ON-THE-SPOT TESTS

In the way that litmus turns red for acid or blue for alkali, research chemists have produced chemical substances that react with body products to give results by color changes on paper strips or wooden sticks. These are useful for rapid tests, such as the sugar in urine that may indicate diabetes, or protein in urine that could suggest a kidney problem. Some blood tests can also be done in just a few minutes.

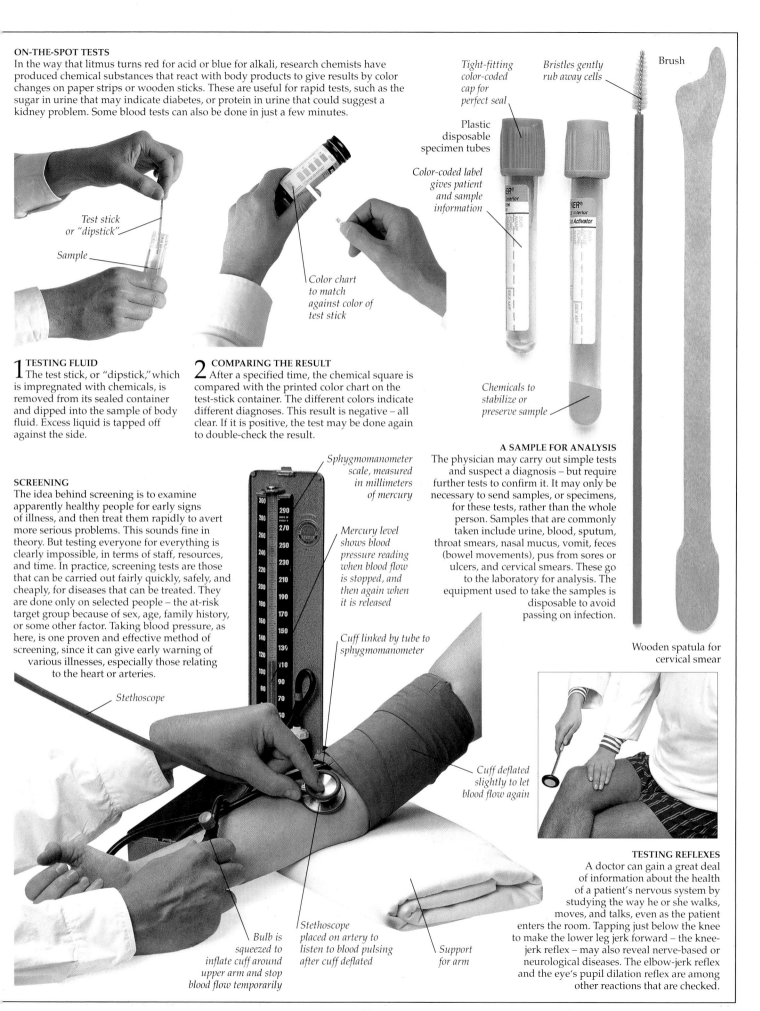

Test stick or "dipstick"

Sample

Tight-fitting color-coded cap for perfect seal

Bristles gently rub away cells

Brush

Plastic disposable specimen tubes

Color-coded label gives patient and sample information

Color chart to match against color of test stick

1 TESTING FLUID
The test stick, or "dipstick," which is impregnated with chemicals, is removed from its sealed container and dipped into the sample of body fluid. Excess liquid is tapped off against the side.

2 COMPARING THE RESULT
After a specified time, the chemical square is compared with the printed color chart on the test-stick container. The different colors indicate different diagnoses. This result is negative – all clear. If it is positive, the test may be done again to double-check the result.

Chemicals to stabilize or preserve sample

A SAMPLE FOR ANALYSIS
The physician may carry out simple tests and suspect a diagnosis – but require further tests to confirm it. It may only be necessary to send samples, or specimens, for these tests, rather than the whole person. Samples that are commonly taken include urine, blood, sputum, throat smears, nasal mucus, vomit, feces (bowel movements), pus from sores or ulcers, and cervical smears. These go to the laboratory for analysis. The equipment used to take the samples is disposable to avoid passing on infection.

Wooden spatula for cervical smear

SCREENING
The idea behind screening is to examine apparently healthy people for early signs of illness, and then treat them rapidly to avert more serious problems. This sounds fine in theory. But testing everyone for everything is clearly impossible, in terms of staff, resources, and time. In practice, screening tests are those that can be carried out fairly quickly, safely, and cheaply, for diseases that can be treated. They are done only on selected people – the at-risk target group because of sex, age, family history, or some other factor. Taking blood pressure, as here, is one proven and effective method of screening, since it can give early warning of various illnesses, especially those relating to the heart or arteries.

Sphygmomanometer scale, measured in millimeters of mercury

Mercury level shows blood pressure reading when blood flow is stopped, and then again when it is released

Cuff linked by tube to sphygmomanometer

Cuff deflated slightly to let blood flow again

Stethoscope

Bulb is squeezed to inflate cuff around upper arm and stop blood flow temporarily

Stethoscope placed on artery to listen to blood pulsing after cuff deflated

Support for arm

TESTING REFLEXES
A doctor can gain a great deal of information about the health of a patient's nervous system by studying the way he or she walks, moves, and talks, even as the patient enters the room. Tapping just below the knee to make the lower leg jerk forward – the knee-jerk reflex – may also reveal nerve-based or neurological diseases. The elbow-jerk reflex and the eye's pupil dilation reflex are among other reactions that are checked.

Into the future

MEDICAL KNOWLEDGE AND PRACTICE have changed beyond recognition over the last century, with surgery and drug therapy becoming increasingly more sophisticated. Another important part of the change has been the rise of a vital branch of medicine called epidemiology. This is concerned with why diseases occur, whom they affect, and how and why they spread or become common in populations. Epidemiology has increasingly made connections between illness and aspects of diet, lifestyle, and environment. In terms of treatment, other areas of science, especially genetic research and biotechnology, promise to bring spectacular advances. But there are still fundamental problems. While thousands of people in rich countries suffer diseases of plenty, such as heart attacks, millions of people in poor regions die from diseases of poverty, such as cholera. What can we do? Is it right to "interfere with nature" and terminate pregnancies, or alter genes? Many amazing medical technologies are available today. However, their use involves complex questions of priorities, morals, ethics, and resources.

A HEALTHY DIET?
In some respects, the human body still belongs to the Stone Age, having evolved to live on a balanced diet of fresh food. But nowadays many foods may lose some of their natural goodness in processing, precooking, and packaging. Research shows that an excess of various substances, such as animal fat and salt, may also be harmful. The blood vessels may become hardened (arteriosclerosis) and blocked with fatty lumps, causing high blood pressure, strokes, and heart attacks.

HEALTHY EXERCISE
The human body has evolved to cope with a fairly active routine, gathering food and escaping from predators. But modern life can be very inactive, sitting in cars, at desks, and in front of the television. This may bring on problems, such as flabby muscles, weak joints, obesity, and an inefficient heart and lungs.
Putting back some of the action with the right types of activity and exercise encourages better health and well-being.

LINKS AND MORE LINKS
Epidemiologists analyze the information gathered about people's health. They explore relationships between illness and what we eat, drink, breathe, and do with our time. They are discovering more and more links. The damage that smoking does to the heart and lungs first came to light like this. Even if the exact process cannot be identified, the links can be revealed, and it seems wise to act on them. Yet millions of people continue to smoke.

INHERITED GENES
DNA forms the long, twisted molecules in cells that constitute genes – chemically coded instructions on how to build and run a body. But there can be mistakes or missing portions in the coding of the 100,000 or so human genes. This can lead to inherited diseases (those running in families) such as cystic fibrosis, Huntington's disease, and hemophilia. As the genes are identified, researchers are finding more diseases, such as diabetes and some cancers, which have genetic links. Identifying the genetic causes may offer hope of better treatment or cure.

Backbone of DNA (sugars and phosphates)

Crosslinks of DNA (nucleotides)

Order of different crosslinks represents the genetic code

Inequality of care

Prevention may be better than cure – but is this practiced on a world scale? Medical needs and expectations vary greatly between developed and less developed countries. The cost of one heart transplant in a hospital in a rich country could bring years of clean water, sanitation, and good food to a whole village in a poor country. These basic facilities are high on the lists of priorities of governments and bodies such as the WHO (World Health Organization), not just for humanitarian and medical reasons, but also for economic ones. The medical costs and the loss of healthy workers are a double burden for agriculture, industry, and trade.

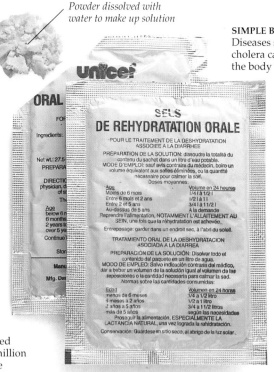

Powder dissolved with water to make up solution

SIMPLE BUT EFFECTIVE
Diseases such as typhoid and cholera cause dehydration when the body loses so many natural fluids, minerals, and salts that life is endangered. In the 1970s an estimated four million children a year died in this way. In 1974 the WHO set up a diarrheal disease control program involving ORT, oral rehydration therapy. This involves replacing the lost water and salts by mouth (orally) with a simple mixture of minerals such as potassium, sodium, and sugar, either made on the spot or using sachets. ORT has been a success in many areas, although one limitation is the lack of clean water for making solutions.

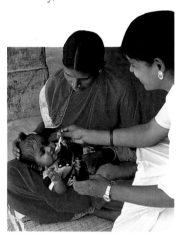

TACKLING DISEASE
Diseases, such as tuberculosis, that have all but disappeared from developed countries still ravage the developing world. One of the most effective weapons is immunization (p. 32), as shown here against polio. Malaria, one of the first recorded diseases, still kills about two million people each year. But a vaccine tested in South America and Africa in the 1990s – the first against a parasitic disease – seems promising. The WHO's campaign to conquer smallpox was successful chiefly through immunization. The disease was declared eradicated in 1979.

STOPPING THE SPREAD
Reusing syringes and needles may save money, but it can be very dangerous. A spot of blood or body fluid from a person with hepatitis, HIV, or a similar infection can spread the disease to many others. Devices such as the Soloshot syringe cannot be refilled after they have been used once. The plunger has a ratchet so that it cannot be pulled out and used again.

Looking ahead

The world community is involved in many medical programs. Priorities include health education, adequate food and good nutrition, safe water and basic sanitation, care for mothers and babies including family planning, prevention and control of local diseases, immunizing against major infective diseases, treatment for injuries and other conditions, and providing enough drugs and medical equipment for treatment. As some diseases are controlled or fade naturally, others seem to replace them. Advances in science and technology are revolutionizing some medical practices and may result in successful treatment for diseases that currently are incurable.

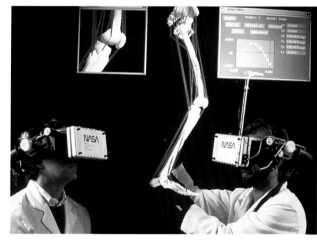

GENE THERAPY
As genetic causes of disease are discovered, the techniques of genetic engineering are being developed to treat them. Possibly, defective genes may be repaired by patching healthy ones into the DNA. This might be done in a group of cells, such as blood cells, which are then injected into the body, hopefully to multiply and replace the diseased cells. However, this might offer only temporary treatment. More controversially, healthy genes may be used to repair defective ones very early in life, in the microscopic fertilized egg or in the very early embryo.

THE COMPUTERIZED PATIENT
Surgeons in training practice on models and cadavers, but they still learn the essentials of their trade on living patients, supervised by a senior surgeon. Virtual reality systems can offer practice. The surgeon sees a computer-generated image in the headset, which is drawn from a "virtual body" in the computer's memory. The dataglove relays the movements of the surgeon's hand to the computer so that it can move aside or cut away the tissues of the computer body.

Index

Acknowledgments

Dorling Kindersley would like to thank:
Stewart Emmens, Simon Chaplin, Neil Irvine, assistant curators, and Graham Wheeldon, conservation assistant, Angela Murphy, photographic marketing manager, and Paul Cox, picture researcher, at the Science Museum, London; Caroline Reed, curator of the Pharmaceutical Museum, London; Costas Diamantopoulos and Jessica Nelson of Omega Technologies, for equipment (pp. 52-53); Grant Kingham of Panasonic Video for the video unit (p. 53); Mary Churchill at Sharplan and Walter Solomon at Litechnica for the laser scalpel (p. 52); Sally Howard, Margaret Dangoor, Barry Fazakerley, and Dr. Ian Fletchel at Roehampton Rehabilitation Center, Queen Mary's

University Hospital for their time and hospital items (pp. 55 and 58); Staff nurse Jo Harris on A Ward; Dr. Ruth Warwick at the North London Blood Transfusion Center for blood products (pp. 50, 57, and 58); Nigel Cope for laboratory items (p. 33); Stephen Whitehead at Glaxo; Lindy McCarthy and James Surtees at Astra Pharmaceuticals; Philip at Porter Nash; Dr. Stephen Curzon; Anthony Wilson for proof reading; Richard Bucknall for photographic assistance; Fiona Wright for the final stages of production; Neville Graham and Nathalie Hennequin for design assistance.

Illustrations Sandie Hill
Index Jane Parker
Additional photography
Andy Crawford, Jo Foord,

Christi Graham, Steve Gorton, Colin Keates, Dave King, S. Price, Andrew McRobb, Nick Nichols, Clive Streeter

Picture credits
t=top b=bottom c=center l=left r=right

Bridgeman Art Library 23tr; /Chelmsford Museum Service 28bl; /Private Collection 36tl; 36cl. British Museum 16tl, 18c, 19c. Bruce Coleman 6tl. e.t. Archive 13tl; 13tr; 15tr; 26bc; 34tl; 49bl; 56br. Mary Evans Picture Library 11cr; 21tl; 25cl; 27tr; 29tl; 34cr; 42tl; 47tl; 48tl; 58tl. Giraudon 9br; 45c; 56tr. Michael Holford 9bl; 17bl. Hulton Deutsch 35bc; 41tc. Images 14cr; 17bc; 22cr; 24tr; 54c. Image Select 30cr; cover and 32bl; 35cr; 37cr; 46cl; 48bl. Katz Pictures Ltd 47cr. Kobal Collection 45tc. Mansell Collection 17br; 26tl. Osterreischische Nationalbibliothek 21tr. Panos 6bl. Pictor 60cl. Popperphoto 42cl. Scala 17tr; 18bl; 19br; 40cl. Science Photo

Library 7tr; 21tc; /Lawrence Migdale 31cr; /Moredun Animal Health 31br; /Martin Dohrn 32tl; /Hank Morgan 33bl; /John Durham 33br; /CNRI 39tr & cr; /James Stevenson 51tr; /Peter Manzell 52br; /Martin Dohr 53br; /Peter Menzel 55tr; /Chris Bjonberg 55bl; 57cr; /Larry Mulvehill 59tl; /Adam Hart 59br; /S. Nagendra 63cl; /Hank Morgan 63bl; /Peter Menzel 63cr. Jean Vertut 8c. Telegraph Colour Library 45cr; /Colorific 57bl. Janine Weidel 47tc. Welcome Centre Medical Photographic Library 31cl. Zefa cover c; 10cl; 10bl; 38tl; 43tl; 45tr; 52c.

With the exception of the items listed above and objects 21cl, 40tl, 40cr, 41cl, 41cr, 41bl, 41br from the Pharmaceutical Museum, London, and 55c from Queen Mary's University Hospital Museum, Roehampton, London, all items are in the collections of the Science Museum, London.